THE FALSE DOCTRINE OF THE FLAT EARTH

A Contextual Biblical Perspective

By David Nikao

"All scripture is given by inspiration of God, and is profitable for doctrine, for reproof, for correction, for instruction in righteousness: That the man of God may be perfect, thoroughly furnished unto all good works."
2 Timothy 3:16-17

The False Doctrine Of The Flat Earth – A Contextual Biblical Perspective is authored and published by David Nikao.

Flat Earth Deception website: www.FlatEarthDeception.com

Copyright 2019 by David Nikao

All rights reserved. No part of this publication may be reproduced, stored in a retrieval system, or transmitted in any form or by any means – electronic, mechanical, digital, photocopy, recording, or any other – except for brief quotations in printed reviews, without prior permission of the author.

ISBN: 978-1686422577
Rev: 082719

Unless otherwise indicated, Scripture quotations are taken from the King James Version of the Bible.

Fair Use of Published Material: This book claims the use of published material under section 107 of the Copyright Act 1976, in which allowance is made for fair use for purposes such as criticism, comment, news reporting, teaching, scholarship, and research. See the Act of 1976 for information.
https://en.wikipedia.org/wiki/Copyright_Act_of_1976

Psalms 19

The heavens declare the glory of God; and the firmament sheweth his handywork. Day unto day uttereth speech, and night unto night sheweth knowledge.

There is no speech nor language, where their voice is not heard. Their line is gone out through all the earth, and their words to the end of the world. In them hath he set a tabernacle for the sun.

Which is as a bridegroom coming out of his chamber, and rejoiceth as a strong man to run a race. His going forth is from the end of the heaven, and his circuit unto the ends of it: and there is nothing hid from the heat thereof.

The law of the LORD is perfect, converting the soul: the testimony of the LORD is sure, making wise the simple. The statutes of the LORD are right, rejoicing the heart: the commandment of the LORD is pure, enlightening the eyes.

The fear of the LORD is clean, enduring for ever: the judgments of the LORD are true and righteous altogether. More to be desired are they than gold, yea, than much fine gold: sweeter also than honey and the honeycomb.

Moreover by them is thy servant warned: and in keeping of them there is great reward. Who can understand his errors? cleanse thou me from secret faults.

Keep back thy servant also from presumptuous sins; let them not have dominion over me: then shall I be upright, and I shall be innocent from the great transgression. Let the words of my mouth, and the meditation of my heart, be acceptable in thy sight, O LORD, my strength, and my redeemer. HalleluYah!

Table Of Contents

Introduction	1
1. My Flat Earth Research Story	4
2. Nathan Roberts Is A Flat Earth Zealot!	6
3. The Flat Earth Causes Division	10
4. The False Dichotomy	12
5. The Proper Context	17
6. Exegesis vs. Eisegesis	18
7. The 240 Flat Earth Verses Debunked	20
8. Earth Created Before the Sun	23
9. Universe is Complete, NOT ever expanding	25
10. Earth Measurements Unknown	26
11. Earth is a Disk/Circle, not a ball	29
12. Earth Measured with a Line, not a curve	42
13. Extremely Large Area of Land is FLAT, no curvature	43
14. A "PLAIN" can't exist on a ball, only a "FLAT " surface	44
15. Paths are Straight, not curved	45
16. Waters are Straight, not curved	50
17. Earthquakes shake Earth and does not move	51
18. Earth is fixed and immovable	53
19. "Be still, and know that I am God."	61
20. Earth has Pillars and hangs on nothing	62
21. Earth has a Face (a geometrical flat surface)	67
22. Waters have a Face (a geometrical flat surface)	76
23. Sky has a Face (a geometrical flat surface)	77
24. Earth has Ends	79
25. Earth has 4 Corners/Quarters	89
26. The Firmament/Dome/Vaulted Dome	97
27. Sun Moves, not the Earth	128
28. Sun STOPS moving	130
29. Sun moves BACKWARDS	133
30. Moon has its own Light	135
31. High Altitude Perspectives	141

Table Of Contents

32. Hell is a bottomless pit at the heart of [flat disc] earth — 143
33. Everyone Sees Jesus — 145
34. New Jerusalem, the HUGE cube — 146
35. "Breadth", spread out FLAT, of the Earth — 149
36. Voice of Creation goes out in a "line" through all the earth — 153
37. Matthews Bible from 1537 says "Flat Earth." — 155
38. Flat Earth Prophecy — 157
39. Creation Worshippers (Heliocentric Sun-god worshippers) — 158
40. Lucifer/Satan's Conspiracy to unite the world — 159
41. God's Word is ALWAYS Faithful and True — 160
42. Flat Earth Verse List Conclusion — 162
43. The Cosmological Gospel Proves The Earth Is A Globe — 165
44. Globe Earth Verses — 176
45. Geocentric Universe Verses — 183
46. Geocentric Earth Findings — 194
47. The Deception About Earth's Orientation — 208
48. The Mindset Of A Flat-Earther — 221
49. Your Conclusion — 225

"I write not these things to shame you, but as my beloved brothers and sisters in Messiah I warn you."
1 Corinthians 4:14

Introduction

Not in my wildest imagination did I think that my first book would be about the flat earth. During the last year, I've been writing a book about prophecy fulfillment, but circumstances pushed this book to the forefront.

When I began this project, I had no idea that writing a book about the Bible verses that flat-earthers cite, would bless me so much. It's been an amazing time of reading Scripture to see the proper context, for in it our Heavenly Father is glorified!

The purpose of this book is to provide a contextual explanation of the verses that flat-earthers cite so that you can judge for yourself. Do the verses describe a flat earth with a dome over it, a heliocentric model with a globe earth revolving around the sun, or a geocentric model with the sun revolving around the globe earth?

It's interesting, and maybe very telling that most flat-earthers don't offer the geocentric model as an option. I think that's intellectually dishonest, especially since it points to a Designer. A balanced discussion about the correct model needs to include it as an option.

Flat-earthers have the mentality that if a verse doesn't fit the heliocentric model, then it must mean that the earth is flat. But the geocentric model also fits many of the verses that they cite.

The enemy has created many deceptions in these end times, and we should be wary of false dichotomies; which is when the enemy causes people to debate between two views that are both a deception, which effectively hides another option that's the truth.

Is that the case here? Read the book with an open mind and decide what makes the most sense.

You'll notice how many things need to be explained away by flat-earthers to make their model seem to fit the description. There are also things which need to be explained away to justify the heliocentric model. Interestingly, in my study of these verses, I've found that the geocentric globe-earth model is the most congruent with Scripture.

The purpose of my Flat Earth Deception website is not to debate scientific explanations, as most everyone does that, and nobody seems to change their mind. My approach is to provide simple, observable proofs; which people can use to determine the shape of the earth.

My method is the same with this book; to provide simple, logical explanations for the context of each verse that flat-earthers cite; to show that they do not prove that the earth is flat with a dome over it.

This book is a Bible study, and I pray that you'll read through the verses and apply discernment as to what each verse is saying. Is it proclaiming that the earth is flat? Or has it been taken out of context by flat-earthers, to make it seem that way?

Some flat-earthers proclaim that the main issue is not the shape of the earth, but it's about whether people can understand the Scriptures. What they're implying is that if you don't believe that the Bible describes a flat earth, then you're not able to comprehend the Scriptures.

If you believe that the earth is flat, then I pray that you'll read the explanations with an open mind. I hope that you want to know the context of the verses which are being cited by flat-earth leaders. I pray that your goal is to know the truth, not just to defend a belief.

Do I think that I'm right about every point? No, of course not, but if you commit to reading the whole book, I believe that you'll see that the collective witness of Scripture refutes that the Bible says that the earth is flat with a dome over it. And I believe that you'll see that many of the supposed flat earth Bible verses actually prove that the earth is a globe.

You may not agree with me, but I sincerely believe what I teach in this book. My explanations aren't perfect, but if you're searching for the truth about the context of the Scriptures that flat-earthers cite, then I'm confident that you'll find it.

If you're going to ridicule me, then do it after you've read all of the explanations in this book. *"Suffer me that I may speak; and after that I have spoken, mock on."* Job 21:3

I'm not going to mock others or question their salvation; just because they believe that the earth is shaped differently than I do. The Bible verse explanations will reveal the truth.

May our Heavenly Father bless you in this study of His Word!

David Nikao

"Grace be to you, and peace, from God our Father, and from the Lord Jesus Christ. Blessed be the God and Father of our Lord Jesus Christ, who hath blessed us with all spiritual blessings in heavenly places in Christ: According as he hath chosen us in him before the foundation of the world, that we should be holy and without blame before him in love."
Ephesians 1:2-4

CHAPTER 1
My Flat Earth Research Story

My primary assignment in these end times is teaching prophecy fulfillment explanations and exposing the many deceptions that the enemy has created. As part of my awakening, I've come to understand many of the deceptions in this world, where everything seems to be fake. Some days it seems like we live in *The Matrix*.

So when people around me started saying that the earth is flat, I took notice. My gut reaction was that it's silly, but I don't want to be misled, so I watched a lot of flat earth videos and read many articles. What I found is that the arguments that they make aren't backed with any science, and they just have CGI-graphics of their flat earth model; which oddly is a 2D projection of the *globe earth*.

My gifting is discernment and logic, but it's not in providing scientific explanations. So I prayed about it, and the Ruach Spirit guided me to simple, observable proofs; which show the shape of the earth. I posted these on my website to share with others.

This is how I came to know a flat-earther named Nathan Roberts as he commented on my website. He gave a link to his flat earth Bible verse list. I read it and was upset as he's misrepresenting the Word.

It doesn't bother me if people think that the earth is flat, but when a Christian proclaims that the Bible says that the earth is flat and they mock others and talk down to them; and they question people's salvation; then I take offense, and I'm compelled to provide a defense of Scripture.

What drives me the most is the stories of people whose lives are being turned upside down by their spouse being a flat-earther. Here's one example of a comment on my website.

"Amen! Amen! Amen! This was so well put together. I agree with you on so many levels! My husband is completely deceived by this whole Flat Earth idea. The past 2 Years of our marriage have been hell, literally! We have 5 small children that I homeschool and the Flat Earth deception has caused so many arguments and confusion within our family. It's so sad to watch Satan work his way in and tear down an entire family unit. I am praying for God to destroy this lie and open my husband's eyes!! It's not just an opinion of my husband's; it's his whole life view. It's all he thinks about. Anyway, thank you so much for all the work you've done! May Yeshua(Jesus) bless you!"

I'm writing this book for people who have family and friends who are flat-earthers; so that they have a Scriptural defense for the design of the earth and universe. I'm writing it for people who are searching out the truth, as more and more people are proclaiming that the earth is flat. I pray that both flat-earthers and globe-earthers will be able to see the truth about what Scripture is describing.

I don't make my prophecy fulfillment websites or YouTube videos about me. I don't post my face all over Facebook, YouTube, my websites, etc.; because the emphasis is on Scriptural truth, and on bringing glory to our Heavenly Father and Messiah; not on me. The same is true for this book. I'm just the servant who is tasked with providing a rebuttal to flat-earthers. The focus is on the Scriptures of our Heavenly Father, which glorify Him.

"Behold, I stand at the door, and knock: if any man hear my voice, and open the door, I will come in to him, and will sup with him, and he with me. To him that overcometh will I grant to sit with me in my throne, even as I also overcame, and am set down with my Father in his throne."
Revelation 3:20-21

CHAPTER 2

Nathan Roberts Is A Flat Earth Zealot!

The reason that I focus so much on Nathan Roberts in this book is that he's the key person in the flat earth community who is proclaiming that there are 240+ Bible verses which describe a flat earth. He's written two books about it, *The Doctrine of the Shape of the Earth – A Comprehensive Biblical Perspective;* and *Earth is FLAT like a MAT!* for kids.

He teaches on his FlatEarthDoctrine Facebook group, YouTube channel, and website. He hands out Flat Earth business cards, which proclaim that he's a *Cosmological Evangelist*. For Nathan, promoting the flat earth model is a business, a way of making money; as he sells books, hats, hoodies, t-shirts, coffee mugs, flyers, business cards, and decals.

Nathan commented on my website, with *"Hey David! Just corrected you via 2 Timothy 3:16-17 on Facebook in this post: DEBUNKING David Nikao, Biblical Flat Earth DENIER. Just want to NOT thank you for taking God's Word OUT OF CONTEXT, and spreading your confusion about God's from yourself to others. I pray you will repent and remove this website immediately. May Yahweh bless your obedience!"*

I obeyed our Heavenly Father alright, in writing this book. 😊

Nathan posted an article on his Flat Earth Doctrine website, saying that my website is geared towards propagating a globe-shaped earth with as many unsubstantiated claims as I can, including Scripture used out of context.

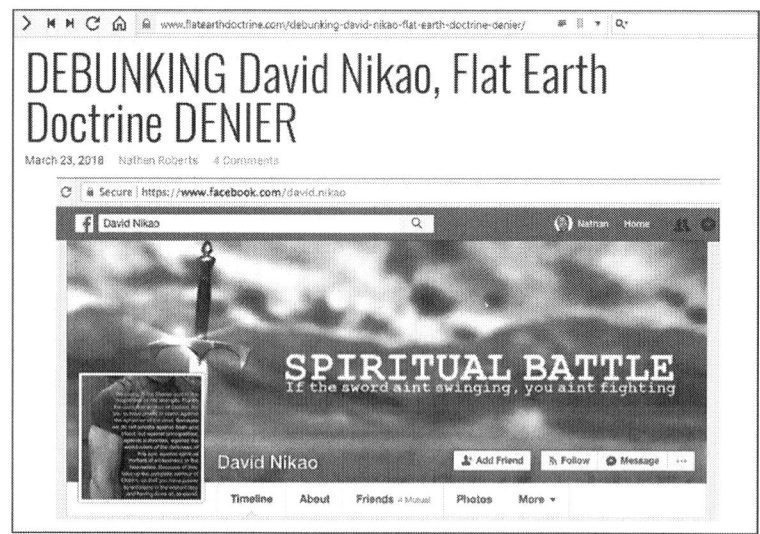

He continued: *"All 240 plus verses point to a stationary and flat earth with a dome over our head. For anyone to state otherwise, and even publish a website, against this biblical truth is quite insane.* **You have to delude God's Word to believe in anything other than a stationary and flat earth when reading God's Word in CONTEXT…which you seem to have a difficult time doing***.*

Your website not only fortifies your own delusion to accepting God's Word as ALWAYS faithful and true, it also leads others in the same direction who are interested in seeking God's Word. You are preach FALSE doctrine in a VERY BOLD way. For those who are attempting to research this topic from a Biblical perspective your website doesn't do any justice to God's Word, it is an embarrassment and a shame.

The confusion you espouse on your website gets absorbed by unsuspecting researchers and then they bring that confusion into their relationships, and that is what causes the division. **Your work is a complete and utter disservice to unity that should be found in God's Word.** *By the way…did you know that water ALWAYS finds level, I know…its profound.*

Oh, and the curvature that should exist is nowhere to be found either on ground or over 100,000 feet in the air (minus Fish-eye lens cameras). **You need to take this website down, repent, and publicly apologize to all people you have steered wrong...otherwise, you are nothing more than a wolf in sheep's clothing from my standpoint.** *May God bless your obedience."*

Keep those statements in mind as you go through Nathan's flat earth Bible verse list. I've repeatedly shared my biblical proofs page with Nathan to consider, and all he's ever done is mock me, call me names, and say that I'm a tool of Satan.

Flat-earthers praise Nathan for sharing the gospel in videos, but the problem is that he's teaching a false gospel. He says that if you don't believe that the earth is flat; then you effectively deny the Scriptures, the Heavenly Father and Messiah. He's directly tying in flat earth beliefs with a person's salvation.

During a recent flat earth debate with YouTuber MCToon (who is a Christian), Nathan Roberts stated *"If a Christian proclaims a globe earth, he too has contradicted his premise that the bible is the inspired word from God. He too will have to reexamine his entire belief system, unless he prefers to remain in his condition by calling God a liar."*

He says things like *"let God be true and every man a liar,"* implying that if you believe that the earth is a globe, then you're calling the Heavenly Father a liar.

He repeatedly says, *"do you unapologetically believe all of God's Word to be Faithful and True?"* which is proclaiming that if you don't agree with his explanations, then you deny that Elohim is faithful and true. He says that if you deny that the Word says that the earth is flat, then you deny Messiah, who is the Word.

This book provides the context of all of the verses that Nathan cites; so that you can decide who has *"deluded God's Word," "preached false doctrine in a very bold way,"* and *"is an embarrassment and a shame."*

Pastor Dean Odle cites Proverbs 18:13 on his website, *"He that answereth a matter before he heareth it, it is folly and shame unto him."* I encourage him and all flat-earthers to read the whole book before making a judgment; for the collective witness of Scripture gives us the complete picture.

"Study to shew thyself approved unto God, a workman that needeth not to be ashamed, rightly dividing the word of truth." 2 Timothy 2:15

We are to let Scripture speak for itself and not inject personal opinion. We should not apply a figurative meaning onto a literal passage, nor apply a literal meaning onto a symbolic passage. And we should not take a passage out of its proper context.

You will see how Nathan Roberts, Pastor Dean Odle, and other flat-earthers; violate those basic rules to promote their beliefs.

*"For I bear them record that they have a zeal of God,
but not according to knowledge."*
Romans 10:2

CHAPTER 3

The Flat Earth Causes Division

I wrote this book because Nathan Roberts, Pastor Dean Odle, Rob Skiba, and others; are on YouTube proclaiming that the Bible teaches that the earth is flat. I wrote this book to educate people about the verses that flat-earthers cite so that they can see that flat-earthers are standing on faulty ground.

There have been many people who have come against me since I started posting my research about the shape of the earth in October 2016. I've been appalled at the language and disposition of Christians who have attacked me. Here are a few examples.

John in Helena, MT said, *"You sure work hard at lying about the scripture and twisting the Word of God into your fallacy of an understanding. May you repent and find the Truth, because you sure don't have it."*

Patricia Gordon said, *"Wow, are you delusional !!!!! You really should go to doctor and have him put you on medicine, for your Schizophrenia because of your comment. It is very apparent you have no idea what you're talking about. Because if you did you would not have made yourself look like a idiot."*

Trisha said, *"Whoever did this so called "facts" to disprove flat earth, is a MORON of all MORONS! It's sooooooooo laughable at the examples you gave because they are taken out of context and more importantly, they have ABSOLUTELY NO SCIENTIFIC PROOF, and I don't mean the JESUIT CONTROLLED FAKE PSEUDO SCIENCE OF NASA, to back it up! YOU ARE A SHILL FOR THE EVIL ELITE and EVIL to the core! In closing, Keep spinning on your ball earth at 1000 mph, as you are being hurled through the universe at a whopping 166, 600 mph (EVEN THOUGH YOUR GOD GIVEN SENSES TELL YOU ARE NOT*

MOVING AT ALL!) and then go worship ALL the demonic, Jesuit, Freemasons, Baal worshipers who came up with the MORONIC and EVIL HELIOCENTRIC model....THEY ARE SUN WORSHIPERS, JUST AS YOU ARE!!!! It's unbelievable that you CLAIM to be a Christian, more like, ANTI Christian!"

Johnny Cirucci, who exposes the deeds of the evil ones, attacked me. He was promoting my prophecy fulfillment studies, and then he read my FlatEarthDeception.com explanations, and he got mad. He said: *"You either work for them* (the Jesuits) *or are demonically deluded. The REALITY of our cosmology undoes the Jesuit discrediting of Scripture and YOU aid them to shore it up. You either consciously wish to shore up the false Jesuit cosmology to discredit the Bible or you're critically, tragically attached to the lie...which doesn't say much for your Walk. We'll see soon enough who was on the side of Christ and His Word. YOU'RE A FRAUD."*

It's interesting that when flat-earthers comment on my website, they don't offer any proof to show me how my explanations are wrong, they only make accusations and call me names.

I've pursued truth, not to defend a belief, and my research has changed my view about what Scripture says about the design of the universe. I believe that the explanations in this book vindicate me from all of the flat-earthers accusations against me. Read the whole book and decide for yourself.

So to Nathan, John, Patricia, Trish, Johnny, and the many people who have come against me, I say thank you! You've inspired me to write this book, which has opened my eyes. I pray that it puts aside the enemy's deception about the earth and universe, so that believers can spend their time where it's most important; in fighting against the enemy with the *rod of iron*, the *sword* of the Scriptures; so that during these end times, many people come into a covenant relationship with the Father through the Son.

CHAPTER 4
The False Dichotomy

In my research, I found that some scientific findings which were published in 2013, showed how the signatures of the universe point back to the earth as the center of all things. Not only do the signatures point to the earth; but they line up with the north-south axis, the equator line, and the ecliptic line. That's very significant, yet the mainstream media has covered it up.

When I look on Facebook, YouTube, and websites; not many people are discussing the Tychonic geocentric earth option; it's only a battle between heliocentric globe-earthers and flat-earthers.

This caused an *'aha!'* moment. What if the enemy has created a false dichotomy, to cause the debate to be between the heliocentric globe earth and the flat earth; so that people ignore the scientific findings of the geocentric globe earth?

If the geocentric globe earth is the true model, then the enemy has done a masterful job at hiding it. They will have hid it by proclaiming that the earth revolves around the sun; which led to the big bang theory, the theory of evolution, etc.; all of which steals glory from our Creator and deceives people. But a geocentric globe earth proves that there's a Designer of the universe and it destroys all of those deceptions.

Interestingly, the Illuminati card game has a Flat Earthers card that says, *"People laugh, but the flat-earthers know something."* What if that *"something"* is that the earth isn't flying through space at 66,000 MPH, orbiting the sun, because it's at the center of the universe? They would be wrong that it's flat, but right that it's not moving.

If you don't know about the Illuminati card game, it was made by the evil ones who foretell events that they cause to happen; as they take control of the world, and push it into a Satanic One World Government. The cards reveal clues about their agenda, as they seem to have a code of ethics, if you will, to foretell their evil plans.

Our earthly perspective of the planets and stars appears the same regardless of whether it's a Copernican heliocentric universe or a Tychonic geocentric universe. There's no way for us to tell the difference, and only people at a very high-level know the truth.

Though people proclaim that the universe is heliocentric, we can't blindly trust those explanations, for in these end-times the enemy controls the scientific world. We'll look to see what Scripture proclaims, for it's our authority.

The Tychonic geocentric earth model was published by Tycho Brahe in the late 16th century. Other geocentric models simply switch the sun and earth, and the planets and the sun revolve in circles around the earth.

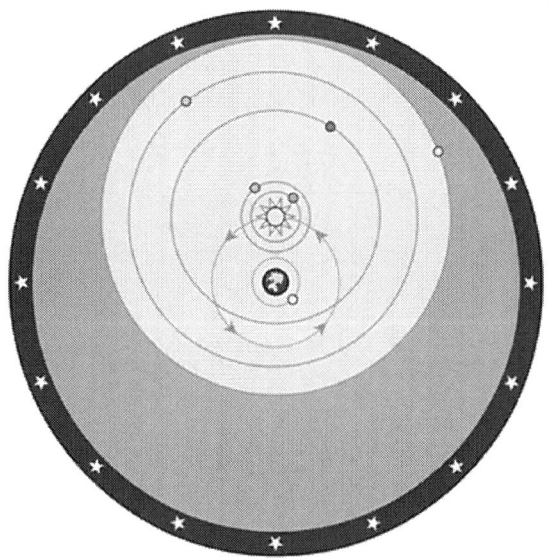

Brahe proposed that the sun is revolving around the earth, and the planets are revolving around the sun. The Tychonic geocentric view explains the retrograde motion of planets.

It wasn't until scientific probes produced data about the radiation of the expanding universe, and the orientation of the quasars and radio galaxies; that researchers were able to see that all of those things were pointing back to Earth as the center of the universe.

These findings were published in a book titled 'Geocentrism 101 – An Introduction into the Science of Geocentric Cosmology' in 2013 and then explained in a movie called *The Principle* in late 2014. Then shortly afterward, the flat earth theory was aggressively pushed on YouTube and Facebook, to cover over the evidence and to cause people to dismiss anyone who teaches a geocentric earth.

If the geocentric globe earth is the truth, then the enemy will have caused flat-earthers to understand some truth, but ultimately be deceived. And they will have caused almost everyone to ignore the geocentric globe earth.

To summarize, I believe that the enemy has created a *false dichotomy* to make the debate between the flat earth and the heliocentric globe earth; so that people don't consider the third option, the geocentric globe earth.

It puts the earth at the center of the universe, proving a Designer/Creator, and explains why stars perfectly circle the Earth; while maintaining the laws of physics of the globe earth and the elaborate surrounding universe, which is a precision time-piece.

I bring this up because as you go through the verses, I want you to keep the geocentric globe earth option in mind; because some verses say that the sun is moving and that the earth is not.

Amazingly, I don't see flat-earthers talking about the geocentric globe earth option; which lacks credibility, as it is a viable explanation. Instead, they like to mock globeheads! Flat-earthers are either being ignorant or intellectually dishonest when they proclaim that the flat earth model is *'geocentric.'*

On Rob Skiba's website, he gives links to these articles: *Arguments for Geocentricity*, *The Scriptural Basis For A Geocentric Cosmology*, *Earth is Stationary Proofs*, *Observations Indicating Geocentrism* and *Current Science Excludes Geocentrism Through Unproven Assumptions*.

He also gives links to the videos *Earth Is Center Of the Whole Universe* by Rick Delano, Geocentrism explained by Rick Delano and Robert Sungenis, and to *The Biblical Geocentric Model - Where Are We In the Universe?* by Philip Stott.

Rob does this to prove that the earth is not moving and that the heliocentric model is wrong, so he concludes that the flat-earth model must be correct. But that's misleading, as those articles are citing a geocentric globe earth, not a flat earth! The scientific experiments prove that the globe earth is the center of the universe and that it's not moving.

Geocentrism is based on a globe earth being at the center of a vast universe. The flat earth model is not geocentric; as the sun, moon, and stars are *inside* the relatively small glass dome. Nothing is revolving *around* the flat earth, only *above* it.

To be fair, in debates with flat-earthers, most Christians who believe in the heliocentric model hardly ever talk about the geocentric universe. That too lacks credibility, as we should look at all options; knowing that the enemy creates deceptions to cause people not to revere the Creator.

The heliocentric model has given rise to explanations of evolution, but the geocentric model destroys that narrative. Just as I asked flat-earthers to pursue truth, not a belief; I'm asking those who believe in the heliocentric model to approach this Bible study with an open mind, to see what Scripture is proclaiming.

"Beloved, believe not every spirit, but try the spirits whether they are of God: because many false prophets are gone out into the world."

1 John 4:1

CHAPTER 5
The Proper Context

Most passages that flat-earthers cite are from the Old Testament, which was written when there wasn't much scientific knowledge about the earth and the universe. They wrote from a simplistic understanding of their knowledge of the geography of the earth, as most of it had not been explored yet.

That some of them presumed that the earth is flat, is not proof that it is flat. If someone lived their whole life in Kansas and had no formal education or access to information; would they presume that the earth is flat? Probably, but that doesn't make it true.

You'll see that most verses that use the word *"earth"* are not pointing to the whole earth, but rather to *"land."* Here are a few examples. Genesis 1:10 defines *earth* as *dry land*. *"And God called the dry land Earth; and the gathering together of the waters called he Seas: and God saw that it was good."* Genesis 1:26 refers to the animals of the sea, air, and earth (*land*), the three parts of the whole earth. *"And God said, Let us make man in our image, after our likeness: and let them have dominion over the fish of the sea, and over the fowl of the air, and over the cattle, and over all the earth, and over every creeping thing that creepeth upon the earth."*

The most problematic thing that people do is 'cherry-pick' verses, which seem to say what they want. They either don't take the time to read the surrounding verses to see the proper context, or they know it and use the verse anyway to promote their beliefs. You'll see that the context of the supposed flat earth verses reveals a very different perspective.

CHAPTER 6
Exegesis vs. Eisegesis

Exegesis is the exposition or explanation of a text, based on careful, objective analysis. The word *exegesis* means *"to lead out of,"* which describes an interpreter being led to his conclusions by following the passage in its proper context.

When you read the whole Bible commentaries of the great theologians (Albert Barnes, Adam Clarke, Jamieson-Fausset-Brown, John Calvin, John Gill, John Wesley, Matthew Henry, Matthew Poole, Thomas Coke, etc.), you don't see them proclaiming that Scripture is declaring that the earth is flat with a dome over it.

The opposite approach to Scripture is *eisegesis*, which is the interpretation of a passage based on a subjective, non-analytical reading. The word *eisegesis* means *"to lead into,"* which describes an interpreter injecting their ideas into the text, making it seem to fit with their beliefs. You'll see that this is what flat-earthers do, as they press their beliefs into the Scriptures, which causes them to take verses out of their proper context.

The Bible is primarily literal, except for parables and prophetic passages which use symbolism to hide the message from those who shouldn't understand it. Our default approach should be to take Scripture literally until proven otherwise by the context.

I say this because both flat-earthers and those who believe in the heliocentric globe earth, tend to proclaim that verses are symbolic when the literal explanation doesn't fit their model.

If Scripture says that the sun is moving and that the earth is fixed and cannot be moved, then why would we not take that literally?

If you answer that it's because scientists teach the heliocentric model, then you're defending man's view, and that's dangerous territory, for we know that the enemy seeks to hide the Creator.

There's a bias by scientists to promote heliocentrism, as geocentrism holds them accountable to a Creator. If the earth is geocentric, we can be sure that the enemy has worked hard to hide that fact, for he seeks to steal glory away from the Creator and to cause people to not believe in Him.

Satan's evil narrative of evolution is based on the heliocentric model. Humanism, the outlook or system of thought attaching prime importance to human rather than divine or supernatural matters, is based on the heliocentric model.

We need to be vigilant so that we don't allow our preconceived beliefs to cause us to miss what Scripture is declaring. We need to let Scripture speak for itself, instead of injecting our beliefs into it. We need to look for the natural explanation that needs no excuses.

"My son, if you receive my words, And treasure my commands within you, So that you incline your ear to wisdom, And apply your heart to understanding; Yes, if you cry out for discernment, And lift up your voice for understanding, If you seek her as silver, And search for her as for hidden treasures; Then you will understand the fear of the Lord, And find the knowledge of God."
Proverbs 2:1-5

CHAPTER 7
The 240 Flat Earth Verses Debunked

Nathan Roberts proclaims that there are 240+ verses which prove that the earth is flat with a dome over it, and he challenges people to provide one verse that says that it's a globe.

Not every flat-earther proclaims that all of these verses prove that the earth is flat, but flat-earth leaders like Rob Skiba teach many of the same verses. I'll add in Rob's teachings when they add to the discussion. If flat earthers disagree with Nathan's verse list, then why are they not speaking out against it?

Nathan's verses and comments are in bold; mine are in regular text. Note that I did not correct spelling and grammar errors in Nathan's text, and I apologize ahead of time for any errors in mine.

In his explanations, Nathan uses both the Hebrew name *"Yahuah"* and the Aramaic name of *"Yahweh"* for our Heavenly Father. The name was revealed to Moses as four Hebrew consonants (*YHUH*) called the Tetragrammaton, and the *'a'* vowel points are added to render it as YaHUaH. Here's how the Tetragrammaton looks in the ancient Hebrew language.

In my explanations, I use the name Yahuah (which is pronounced Yah-oo-ah) for our Heavenly Father. He breathed life into us, which you can mimic when you inhale with your mouth saying "Yah" and exhale with "oo-ah."

HalleluYah means *"praise Yah!"* Praise our Heavenly Father!

Here's Nathan's introduction about his list of verses, which are available on his website.

Bible says "Flat Earth!" Did you know there are 240+ Bible verses that reveal earth as being stationary and flat with a dome overhead?

NOTE: When performing my study I did not limit my research to any 1 particular English translation Bible. Rather, I compared multiple English translated Bibles to come to my conclusions. Furthermore, I studied the original Hebrew and Greek words to be more certain of my study, and encourage everyone to do likewise.

What that means is that instead of using one good translation, he looked for translations which read how he wants; to make it seem like the verse is pointing to a flat earth with a dome over it. As for his knowledge of the Hebrew and Greek words, we'll see how well he did.

I've used the King James, as it's a good translation which is well-known. I also reference the King James 3 (KJ3) Literal Translation Bible, which was written by J.P. Green, who wrote the four-volume Hebrew/Greek/English Interlinear Bible; as it provides insight.

Nathan continues: I'll also cite the following Bible Dictionaries when they add to the discussion: The 1828 Webster's Dictionary of the English language is based upon the King James Bible. Easton's Bible Dictionary (1897) contains 4,000 entries relating to the Bible, from a 19th century Christian viewpoint. Naves Topical Index (1896) is a topical concordance of the Bible, and contains Biblical references to over 20,000 topics. Smith's Bible Dictionary (1863) is a comprehensive A to Z glossary of Biblical names, concepts, places, objects, and technical terms.

The Brown-Driver-Briggs Hebrew and English Lexicon (1906) from eminent Hebrew Bible scholars Francis Brown, R. Driver, and Charles Briggs; who spent over twenty years researching, writing, and preparing this work.

Nathan cites those resources to try to give his explanations credibility, but the irony is that none of those esteemed scholars proclaim that the earth is flat with a dome over it.

You're going to see that none of the 240 verses that are cited by Nathan Roberts prove that the earth is flat with a dome over it, many of them have nothing to do with the shape of the earth, and some of them actually prove that the earth is a globe.

You'll see that Nathan has taken these Bible verses out of context, some so badly that it's both funny and sad.

"For the time will come when they will not endure sound doctrine, but according to their own desires, because they have itching ears, they will heap up for themselves teachers; and they will turn their ears away from the truth, and be turned aside to fables."
2 Timothy 4:3-4

CHAPTER 8
Earth Created Before the Sun

Nathan cites Genesis 1:1-19

These verses give the creation account of the first four days. Nathan proclaims that if the universe is centered on the sun, then it would make sense to create the sun first, and then the planets which circle it. That seems logical, but it doesn't prove that the earth is flat; as the geocentric globe earth could have been created first, and then the sun and moon which revolve around it.

The vast creation of the earth and all that's on it and around it, are described in thirty-one verses. We have to keep in mind that many details were left out.

In my study of Genesis 1, I noticed something really interesting. Read Genesis 1:1-4, *"In the beginning God created the heaven and the earth. And the earth was without form, and void; and darkness was upon the face of the deep. And the Spirit of God moved upon the face of the waters. And God said, Let there be light: and there was light. And God saw the light, that it was good: and God divided the light from the darkness."*

The sun wasn't created until the fourth day, so what was the "*light*" that illuminated the earth on the first day? It's interesting that when you read John 1:1-5, which points to Messiah, it's about the *beginning* and *light*. *"In the beginning was the Word, and the Word was with God, and the Word was God. The same was in the beginning with God. All things were made by him; and without him was not any thing made that was made. In him was life; and the life was the light of men. And the light shineth in darkness; and the darkness comprehended it not."*

Messiah declared that He's the light of the world. *"Then spake Jesus again unto them, saying, I am the light of the world: he that followeth me shall not walk in darkness, but shall have the light of life."* John 8:12

The Apostle Paul said in 2 Corinthians 4:6, *"For God, who commanded the light to shine out of darkness, hath shined in our hearts, to give the light of the knowledge of the glory of God in the face of Jesus Christ."*

Messiah is *the light of the world* who has shined upon the earth from the first day of creation. HalleluYah!

"Who hath delivered us from the power of darkness, and hath translated us into the kingdom of his dear Son: In whom we have redemption through his blood, even the forgiveness of sins: Who is the image of the invisible God, the firstborn of every creature: For by him were all things created, that are in heaven, and that are in earth, visible and invisible, whether they be thrones, or dominions, or principalities, or powers: all things were created by him, and for him."
Colossians 1:13-16

CHAPTER 9

Universe is Complete, NOT ever expanding

Nathan cites Genesis 2:1 *"Thus the heavens and the earth were finished, and all the host of them."*

Nathan is making the point that the creation of the earth is *finished*, which he says means that it's not still expanding. By this logic, he asserts that this proves that the earth is flat with a dome over it.

The Hebrew word for "finished" is 3615 kalah; to end, whether intransitive (to cease, be finished, perish) or transitived (to complete, prepare, consume):—accomplish, cease, consume (away), determine, destroy (utterly), be (when ... were) done, (be an) end (of), expire, (cause to) fail, faint, finish, fulfil, fully, have, leave (off), long, bring to pass, wholly reap, make clean riddance, spend, quite take away, waste.

The same word, kalah, is used in the next verse to mean ended, "And on the seventh day God ended his work which he had made; and he rested on the seventh day from all his work which he had made." Genesis 2:2

The text is saying that the work of creation was *completed* (*ended*) after the six days. Can Yahuah not create a universe which continues to expand, even after He *finished* His work? Yes!

Even if the universe is not expanding as NASA proclaims, that doesn't prove that the earth is flat; as that can also be true with a globe earth. This is a great example of Nathan pushing his beliefs onto the text, to make it seem to proclaim that the earth is flat.

"And ye are complete in him, which is the head of all principality and power."
Colossians 2:10

CHAPTER 10
Earth Measurements Unknown

Nathan cites Job 38:4-5, Job 38:18, Jeremiah 31:37, Proverbs 25:3

Nathan is proclaiming that because measurements of the earth were unknown, that the earth must be flat. Visualize a domed earth, which is limited in size. Could the size not be measured? Yes! Now visualize an enormous universe that may still be expanding. Can it be measured? That's debatable.

These verses emphasize the complex creation of Yahuah, of which no man can fully comprehend.

Job 38:4-5 *"Where wast thou when I laid the foundations of the earth? Declare, if thou hast understanding. Who hath laid the measures thereof, if thou knowest? or who hath stretched the line upon it?"*

Nathan proclaims that a *stretched line* can't be used on a round globe earth, but only on a flat earth; as he believes that all lines are straight. But a circle is made out of a curved line, as we see with this smiley face. 😊

The Strong's Hebrew word for *"stretched"* is Hebrew 5186 *natah*; to bend away and to bow: *to stretch or spread out; by implication, to bend away (including moral deflection).* The Strong's Hebrew word for *"line"* is 6957 *qav; from 6960 (compare 6961);* a cord *(as connecting), especially for measuring; figuratively, a rule. Hebrew 6961 qaveh;* a (measuring) cord *(as if for binding):—line.*

It's describing a cord that's used especially for measuring. Does a cord bend? Yes! Can we not wrap a measuring cord around a basketball to measure its circumference? Yes!

The Webster's 1828 Dictionary defines the word *circumference* as <u>*The line that bounds a circle*</u>; <u>*the exterior line of a circular body*</u>; *the whole exterior surface of a round body; a periphery.*

Nathan proclaims to be knowledgeable about the Hebrew words, so how does he not see that the words *"stretched the line"* are pointing to a *measuring cord*, which can be used to determine the size of round objects?

Job 38:18 *"Hast thou perceived the breadth of the earth? declare if thou knowest it all."*

It's declaring that man cannot comprehend all of the facts of the created earth. The irony of Nathan citing this verse is that we know the width of the globe earth, but flat-earthers can't tell you the width of their proposed flat earth because they haven't measured it.

I'm not talking about estimating the size based on the supposed flat earth map; I'm referring to *boots on the ground* measurements which prove it out with a theodolite, which is a precision optical instrument for measuring angles between designated visible points in the horizontal and vertical planes.

Jeremiah 31:37 *"Thus saith the LORD; if heaven above can be measured, and the foundations of the earth searched out beneath, I will also cast off all the seed of Israel for all that they have done, saith the LORD."*

The heavens of the flat earth model are limited, as they're under a dome, which could be measured. With all of our advanced technology, a strong laser could be used to shine up to the dome to measure its height.

The heavens that surround the globe earth are vast, and it's debatable if they can be measured. This is not a flat earth proof, and it seems to prove the opposite of what Nathan implies.

The context of the verse is not about the design of the universe; but that Yahuah is declaring that it's impossible that He will cast off all the seed of Israel. Interestingly, two verses later Yahuah proclaims that a *measuring line* is to be used outside the city of Jerusalem, for the hill of lepers. *"And the measuring line shall yet go forth over against it upon the hill Gareb, and shall compass about to Goath."* Jeremiah 31:39

Proverbs 25:3 *"The heaven for height, and the earth for depth, and the heart of kings is unsearchable."*

This verse is describing the very opposite of a limited-space domed flat-earth, as it points to a universe which has heavens that are so expansive that they're unsearchable.

It's pointing to the wisdom of kings not being fathomed by the common people. Did the Israelites understand the wisdom of King Solomon? No, the height and depth of his wisdom were beyond their comprehension.

Ironically, the previous verse proclaims, *"It is the glory of God to conceal a thing: but the honor of kings is to search out a matter."* As you read through the verses in this book, you'll see that flat-earthers haven't searched out the matter, as they've taken verses out of context. Indeed, it is an honor to search out the truth and give a proper explanation.

These verses about the measurements of the earth and heavens being unknown, don't prove that the earth is flat, and they seem to point to a globe earth with a vast universe.

"And we have known and believed the love that God hath to us. God is love; and he that dwelleth in love dwelleth in God, and God in him."
1 John 4:16

CHAPTER 11
Earth is a Disk/Circle, not a ball

Nathan cites Isaiah 40:22, Proverbs 8:27, Job 38:13-14

Isaiah 40:22 *"It is he that sitteth upon the circle of the earth, and the inhabitants thereof are as grasshoppers; that stretcheth out the heavens as a curtain, and spreadeth them out as a tent to dwell in."*

Isaiah 40:22 is a key verse that flat-earthers cite. They proclaim that Isaiah knows the difference between a *"ball"* and a *"circle,"* so if he were describing a globe earth, then he would have used the word *ball*, not *circle*.

The Strong's Hebrew for the word *"circle"* is 2329 *chuwg*; which means *a circle:—circle, circuit, compass*. The Strong's Hebrew word for *"ball"* is 1754, *duwr*; which means *a circle, ball or pile:—ball, turn, round about*.

The word *ball* is used in Isaiah 22:18, *"He will surely violently turn and toss thee like a ball into a large country: there shalt thou die, and there the chariots of thy glory shall be the shame of thy lord's house."*

It's interesting that flat-earthers only give two options for Isaiah to use; a *circle* and a *ball*. Rob Skiba proclaims, *"Circle means circle. Not ball. Isaiah knows the difference between a circle and a spherical object. Note that a few chapters prior he uses a completely different word for a ball."*

Rob cites the International Standard Version of Isaiah 40:22 to promote his beliefs, as it uses the word *disc*, *"He's the one who sits above the disk of the earth, and its inhabitants are like grasshoppers. He's the one who stretches out the heavens like a curtain, and spreads them like a tent to live in."*

Nathan says that *"it's a fact that most adults do not understand concepts about basic shapes,"* but it seems that he doesn't understand them. There's a difference between a circle and a disk. A circle is a curved line, which has no area - just as a straight line has no area. A disk, however, is a round portion of a plane which has a circular outline.

If you draw a circle on a sheet of metal and cut it out, the round piece is a disk. There's material in the middle of the circle, and it has height.

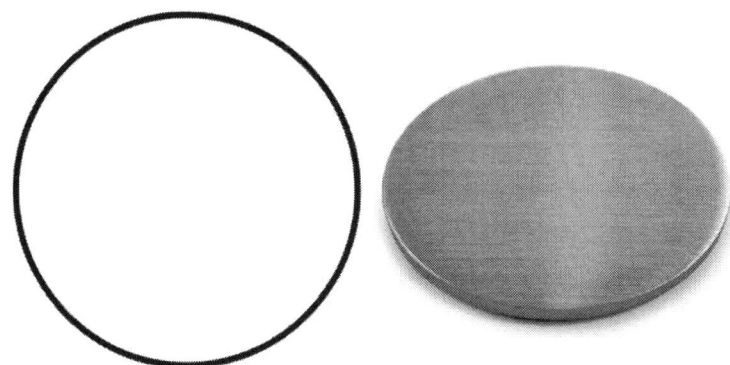

Despite flat-earthers only giving the two options of *circle* and *ball*, there's another Hebrew word that Isaiah could have used if he wanted to describe a flat disc earth, the word *"round."* The Strong's Hebrew for the word *"round"* is 5696 `agol; which means: *to revolve, circular:—round.*

These verses use the word *"round"* to describe a 3D disc with height, which seems like a much better fit to describe a disc earth.

"And he made a molten sea, ten cubits from the one brim to the other: it was <u>round all about, and his height was five cubits</u>: and a line of thirty cubits did compass it round about." 1 Kings 7:23

"And in the top of the base was there a <u>round compass of half a cubit high</u>: and on the top of the base the ledges thereof and the borders thereof were of the same." 1 Kings 7:35

"Also he made a molten sea of ten cubits from brim to brim, <u>round in compass, and five cubits the height thereof</u>; and a line of thirty cubits did compass it round about." 2 Chronicles 4:2

The point I'm making is that Isaiah didn't use the word *"round,"* which is the better word to describe a disk-shaped flat earth. And he didn't use the word *"ball,"* which points to a globe-shaped earth. He used the word *"circle"* for a reason, as he is not describing the earth itself.

Isaiah 40:22 doesn't say *"circular earth,"* it says *"the circle of the earth."* The *circle* is the focus, not the earth. Just like you would say *'the ring of Saturn'* to point to the ring, not the planet; Isaiah is pointing to the *circle*, not the earth. The context of the verse shows that he's pointing to the *ecliptic circle* in the *expanse* of the heavens, which surrounds the globe earth.

Seeing this was an *'aha!'* moment for me and I hope for you because it changes the whole debate about this verse; as the *circle* surrounds the globe earth, which is a validation of the globe earth model.

Isaiah 40:22 says, *"It is he that sitteth upon the circle of the earth."* The *'he'* is our Heavenly Father, who is not sitting upon the earth; so right there, we can see that the *circle* is not describing the earth.

Isaiah 40:22 declares *"and the inhabitants thereof are as grasshoppers,"* which reveals that Yahuah's viewpoint makes people look small, so we can see that He's high above the earth; once again proving that He's not sitting on a flat circle earth or a globe earth.

It's proclaiming that the Father is in the heavens, so why are flat-earthers imagining that He is sitting on a circle earth? *"Why do the heathen rage, and the people imagine a vain thing? He that sitteth in the heavens shall laugh: the Lord shall have them in derision."* Psalms 2:1, 4

Isaiah 40:22 says, *"that stretcheth out the heavens as a curtain, and spreadeth them out as a tent to dwell in."* The constellations on the ecliptic *"circle"* give the primary message of the redemption story.

Above and below those twelve primary constellations are the thirty-six decan constellations, which are *spread out* as a *curtain* to the north and south celestial poles, which is like a *tent* that encloses the earth, a spherical *tabernacle* of stars, in which Yahuah dwells.

The word for *"tent"* is 168 *'ohel*; which means: *a tent:—covering, (dwelling)(place), home, tabernacle.*

Yahuah's home is in the *tabernacle* of stars which surrounds the globe earth as a *curtain*. The forty-eight constellations of the mazzaroth which are based around the ecliptic *circle*, have proclaimed His plan of redemption from the beginning. They witness to us every night.

The context of Isaiah 40:22 is the stars of heaven, not the earth. Yahuah is pointing to the *Gospel in the Stars*, which the enemy has perverted with explanations of pagan gods.

Here are brief explanations of the twelve primary constellations:
Virgo represents *the seed of the woman, Messiah the Incarnate Son.*
Libra represents *the required price, Messiah the Redeemer.*
Scorpio represents *the mortal conflict, Messiah the Sufferer.*
Sagittarius represents *the final triumph, Messiah the Conqueror.*

Capricorn represents *life out of death, Messiah the Sacrifice.*
Aquarius represents *blessing out of victory, Messiah the Living Water.*
Pisces represents *deliverance out of bondage, Messiah the Liberator.*
Aries represents *glory out of humiliation, Messiah the Crowned Lamb.*

Taurus represents *His glorious coming, Messiah the Judge.*
Gemini represents *His rule on Earth, Messiah the King.*
Cancer represents *His possessions held secure, Messiah the Protector.*
Leo represents *His enemies destroyed, Messiah the Victor.*
HalleluYah!

Zodiac comes from the Greek *zodiakos*, which means 'a circle.'

I'm not talking about the false teaching of astrology horoscopes that are based on the zodiac, but theology which is proclaimed by it.

Job understood that the constellations told the story of his redemption, and he mentioned them by name. *"Which maketh Arcturus, Orion, and Pleiades, and the chambers of the south."* Job 9:9

"Canst thou fasten the bands of the Pleiades, or loosen the cords of Orion? Dost thou bring forth the constellations each in its season? Or dost thou guide the Bear with her sons? Knowest thou the ordinances of the heavens? dost thou determine their rule over the earth?" Job 38:31-33

Amos 5:8 points to the constellation Orion, *"Seek him that maketh the seven stars and Orion, and turneth the shadow of death into the morning, and maketh the day dark with night: that calleth for the waters of the sea, and poureth them out upon the face of the earth: The LORD is his name."*

Each of the twelve signs pictorially represents a prophetic event about the story of salvation. There are three decan constellations for each of the twelve primary ones, so there's forty-eight total.

An example is Orion, which is a decan of Taurus the bull. It means *Coming As Light*, and since creation, it has foretold a mighty person who is to come to earth, who triumphs over the great enemy of mankind, who takes away sin and its disastrous effects, and who brings in blessing and righteousness. It points to our Messiah.

In the book of Revelation, Messiah proclaimed to be the *Alpha and Omega*, the *beginning* and the *end*, the *first and the last*. *Alpha* and *Omega* are the first and last letters of the Greek alphabet.

In the Hebrew language, the first and last letters are the *Aleph and Tav*. The Hebrew language uses symbols as well, and the symbol for the letter *Aleph* is the head of a bull/ox, which points to a strong leader. The symbol for the letter *Tav* is the cross, which points to a *mark*, a *sign*, and a *covenant*.

Are you seeing how the symbols of the constellations match the symbols of the Hebrew language and are pointing to the promised Messiah? Our mighty leader came to defeat the enemy by His sacrifice on the cross, which ratified the everlasting covenant with His blood. HalleluYah!

Let's back up to get the context of Isaiah 40:22. Yahuah is declaring the glory of His creation. *"To whom then will ye liken God? or what likeness will ye compare unto him? The workman melteth a graven image, and the goldsmith spreadeth it over with gold, and casteth silver chains."* Isaiah 40:18-19

Yahuah is pointing to the *circle* of stars, which have declared the Gospel message from creation. *"Have ye not known? have ye not heard? hath it not been told you from the beginning? have ye not understood from the foundations of the earth?"* Isaiah 40:21

We see that Yahuah tells Isaiah to look up to the *circle* of the stars (*host*) of the mazzaroth. *"Lift up your eyes on high, and behold who hath created these things, that bringeth out their host by number: he calleth them all by names by the greatness of his might, for that he is strong in power; not one faileth."* Isaiah 40:26

Here are a few examples of the stars being named, all of which point to Messiah: Spica means *the Branch*. Arcturus means *He comes*. Pollux means *who comes to suffer*. Antares means *the wounded*. Sirius means *the Prince*. Elnath means *slain*. Procyon means *the Redeemer*. Vega means *He shall be exalted*. Regulus means *regal, the King Star*. HalleluYah!

The same Hebrew word for *"circle"* in Isaiah 40:22 is used in Job 22:14 to describe the *circuit of heaven*, again proclaiming that Yahuah walks on the *circle of heaven*, not on a circle flat earth. *"Thick clouds are a covering to him, that he seeth not; and he walketh in the circuit (chuwg) of heaven."*

Rob Skiba cites the Holman Christian Standard Bible for Job 22:14, *"Clouds veil Him so that He cannot see, as He walks on the circle of the sky."* It says that He walks on the *"circle of the sky,"* not a circle-shaped earth. How are you missing this Rob?

This key verse that flat-earthers cite is a proof of the globe earth. They may proclaim that the ecliptic circle could exist above the flat earth, but Yahuah is not walking on the circuit of heaven under a glass dome. And flat-earthers have no scientific explanations for how the sun, moon, and constellations move about in perfect sequence under a glass dome.

With the understanding that Isaiah 40:22 is pointing to the ecliptic circle, which has proclaimed the Gospel message since creation; let's look at Psalms 19:1-6 with fresh eyes.

"The heavens declare the glory of God; and the firmament sheweth his handywork. Day unto day uttereth speech, and night unto night sheweth knowledge. There is no speech nor language, where their voice is not heard. Their line is gone out through all the earth, and their words to the end of the world. In them hath he set a tabernacle for the sun, Which is as a bridegroom coming out of his chamber, and rejoiceth as a strong man to run a race. His going forth is from the end of the heaven, and his circuit unto the ends of it: and there is nothing hid from the heat thereof."

Messiah, the *Sun of Righteousness* (Malachi 4:2), is symbolized by the sun, which moves in a circuit through the twelve constellations every year, to proclaim the Gospel message. How glorious is that?

Satan perverted the story of the constellations to make them about pagan gods, which causes people to worship many false gods, including the pagan sun and moon gods.

And sadly, Satan has done a great job at covering over the truth of the constellations, by causing Pastors and believers to dismiss all study of the stars.

Every night they declare the Gospel story of Messiah overcoming the enemy and redeeming the set-apart saints. HalleluYah!

I contacted Robert Sungenis after I attended the 2018 Flat Earth Conference debate between him and Rob Skiba, and shared my perspective about the *circle* of Isaiah 40:22; but once you believe a certain narrative; it's hard to change your view.

Isaiah 40:22 is not a flat earth proof, and I consider the explanation of it and Job 22:14 to be proofs that the earth is a globe, as the ecliptic *circle* surrounds the globe earth.

Proverbs 8:27 *"When he prepared the heavens, I was there: when he set a compass upon the face of the depth."*

Nathan seems to be proclaiming that the compass, the *"circle,"* is an ice wall that supposedly surrounds the flat earth to contain the water of the oceans. But the verse is proclaiming that Yahuah inscribed a compass *"upon"* the deep waters, not *"around"* them.

Proverbs 8:28 continues the description, *"When he established the clouds above: when he strengthened the fountains of the deep."* These two verses both feature the heavens and clouds in the first part and the deep waters in the second part. The KJ3 Literal Translation Bible reads, *"In His preparing the heavens, I was there; in His decreeing a circle on the face of the deep. In His forming the clouds above, in His making the strong springs of the deep."*

Job 26:10 is saying the same thing, *"He hath compassed (chuwg) the waters with bounds until the day and night come to an end."* Job is saying that the water under the earth will stay there until all is fulfilled, for Yahuah promised never to use the fountains of the deep to flood the earth again.

Psalms 24:1-2 says that the earth is founded, set upon, the deep seas, the fountains of the deep, from which the floodwaters came, and then returned. *"The earth is the LORD'S, and the fulness thereof; the world, and they that dwell therein. For he hath founded it upon the seas, and established it upon the floods."*

This matches with the narrative of Genesis 1:9-10, as the earth was covered in water until Yahuah commanded much of the water to be bound under the earth. *"And God said, Let the waters under the heaven be gathered together unto one place, and let the dry land appear: and it was so. And God called the dry land Earth; and the gathering together of the waters called he Seas: and God saw that it was good."*

And it matches the narrative in Psalms 104:5-9, which says that the deep waters are bound. *"Who laid the foundations of the earth, that it should not be removed for ever. Thou coveredst it with the deep as with a garment: the waters stood above the mountains. At thy rebuke they fled; at the voice of thy thunder they hasted away. They go up by the mountains; they go down by the valleys unto the place which thou hast founded for them. <u>Thou hast set a bound that they may not pass over; that they turn not again to cover the earth</u>."*

It seems that the *"circle"* is the upper layers of the globe earth, which is over vast reserves of water. Geologists believe that a layer of a mineral called *ringwoodite*, which is found 400 miles beneath the Earth's surface, may hold three times the amount of water found in Earth's oceans. Massive volcanic activity may have affected these deep underground reservoirs, to cause them to be released and flood the earth.

Yahuah is proclaiming that He controls every detail of our world, from the heavens to the depth of the waters below the earth. He controls the great flow of water, as it completes its cycle coming down by precipitation and back up again by evaporation.

Proverbs 8:27 is not proof that the earth is flat, and it seems to point to a globe earth. How would a compass, a circle, be inscribed *over* the vast reservoir of water under a flat earth? It's really easy to see how a circular barrier covers over the vast underground sea of water, with the layers under the globe earth.

Job 38:13-14 *"That it might take hold of the ends of the earth, that the wicked might be shaken out of it? It is turned as clay to the seal, and they stand as a garment."*

Kings use seals and signet rings with a unique design, to stamp their mark on the wax seal of a letter, to make sure that nobody opens it before it's delivered. Nathan is proclaiming that the earth was like a flat surface of clay on which Yahuah used a seal to form the shape of the flat earth, the mountains, lands masses, etc. When you press down on the material, the excess is squeezed out to the side. Flat-earthers say that this raised outside edge is the ice wall which surrounds the flat earth, to contain the water.

Based on that logic, wouldn't the outside edge be made up of excess earth (land) which was pressed out, instead of ice? And do we really think that our Creator made a gigantic signet ring to form the clay of a vast flat earth? No, I don't think so.

That aside, Job 38:14 does not say *"It was turned as clay to the seal"* to point back to a creation event, it says *"It is turned as clay to the seal"* to describe an active event.

So what's the context of the verse? What does it describe before the *earth is turned as clay to the seal*? It describes wicked men! Did they exist before the creation of the earth? No, so we can invalidate flat-earthers claim because it's clearly stating that wicked men existed before the *earth is turned as clay to the seal*.

Read Job 38:12-20, and you notice that the context is about *light*. The verses include the words: *morning, dayspring, light is withheld, shadow, where light dwelleth,* and *darkness*; and it mentions *"wicked men"* twice. It is declaring that the Earth is changed; that it's transformed, as the sun removes the darkness.

The context is the light hitting the earth, as Job 38:12 is talking about the morning and dawn knowing its place. *"Hast thou commanded the morning since thy days, and caused the dayspring to know his place."* As the sun rises and brings light on the earth, the deeds of the wicked are exposed. *"That it might take hold of the ends of the earth, that the wicked might be shaken out of it?"* Job 38:13

Job 24:13-17 describes exactly that. *"They are of those that rebel against the light; they know not the ways thereof, nor abide in the paths thereof. The murderer rising with the light killeth the poor and needy, and in the night is as a thief. The eye also of the adulterer waiteth for the twilight, saying, No eye shall see me: and disguiseth his face. In the dark they dig through houses, which they had marked for themselves in the daytime: they know not the light. For the morning is to them even as the shadow of death: if one know them, they are in the terrors of the shadow of death."*

John 3:19-21 proclaims that evil men love darkness *"And this is the condemnation, that light is come into the world, and men loved darkness rather than light, because their deeds were evil. For every one that doeth evil hateth the light, neither cometh to the light, lest his deeds should be reproved. But he that doeth truth cometh to the light, that his deeds may be made manifest, that they are wrought in God."*

Ephesians 5:11-13 points to light exposing the deeds of evil *"And have no fellowship with the unfruitful works of darkness, but rather reprove them. For it is a shame even to speak of those things which are done of them in secret. But all things that are reproved are made manifest by the light: for whatsoever doth make manifest is light."*

Adam Clarke's Commentary on the Bible (1826) says this about Job 38:13-14: *The meaning appears to be this: as soon as the light begins to dawn upon the earth, thieves, assassins, murderers, and adulterers, who all hate and shun the light, fly like ferocious beasts to their several dens and hiding places; for such do not dare to come to the light, lest their works be manifest, which are not wrought in God.*

John Gill's Exposition of the Whole Bible (1763) says this about Job 38:14: *As the clay receives a different form by the impress of the seal upon it, so the earth appears in a different manner by the spring of morning light upon it; in the darkness of the night nothing of its form and beauty is to be seen.*

Matthew Poole's Commentary on the Holy Bible (1685) says about Job 38:13-14: *Shaken out of it, from the face of the earth. And this effect the morning light hath upon the wicked, partly because it discovers them, and drives them into their lurking holes.*

Job 38:15 is speaking about light being withheld: *"And from the wicked, their light is withholden, and the high arm shall be broken."* It's saying that the deeds of the wicked ones become exposed in the light so that their power and strength is broken.

It's fascinating that flat-earthers can read Job 38:13-14 and not see that it's proclaiming that *"wicked men"* existed before the *"earth is turned as clay to the seal,"* which invalidates that it's pointing to a creation event.

The danger of a belief system is that it can cause people to ignore the context. Now every time you see someone point to the seal in Job 38:13-14 forming a flat earth, you know that it's talking about light exposing the deeds of evil men who love darkness.

"If ye then be risen with Christ, seek those things which are above, where Christ sitteth on the right hand of God. Set your affection on things above, not on things on the earth.
Philippians 2:6-10

CHAPTER 12

Earth Measured with a Line, not a curve

Nathan cites Job 38:4-5 *"Where wast thou when I laid the foundations of the earth? declare, if thou hast understanding. Who hath laid the measures thereof, if thou knowest? or who hath stretched the line upon it?"*

I addressed this in the previous *Earth Measurements Unknown* section. The word for *line* is Hebrew 6957 *qav* from 6960; which means <u>a cord</u>, *especially for measuring; figuratively, a rule.* The word *qav* is pointing to a *measuring cord*. Does a cord bend? Yes!

A circle is made out of a curved line, as not all lines are straight like Nathan implies. Can we not wrap a measuring cord around a basketball, to measure its circumference? Yes, so we can see that a ball/globe can be measured with a curved line, which invalidates Nathan's premise.

There's some insight and humor in verses like Ezekiel 42:16-1, which use the term *"round about"* when measuring a square area. *"He measured the east side with the measuring reed, five hundred reeds, with the measuring reed round about. He measured the north side, five hundred reeds, with the measuring reed round about."*

Saying that the *earth is measured with a line, not a curve* is nonsensical. Flat-earthers, how do you defend Job 38:4-5 being on the list, as it points to a *cord* which can be *stretched* around a *curved surface* to measure it?

CHAPTER 13

Extremely Large Area of Land is FLAT, no curvature

Nathan cites Ezekiel 45:1, which he says represents a length of approximately 52 miles and a width of approximately 20 miles without any CURVATURE, only FLAT.

"Moreover, when ye shall divide by lot the land for inheritance, ye shall offer an oblation unto the LORD, an holy portion of the land: the length shall be the length of five and twenty thousand reeds, and the breadth shall be ten thousand. This shall be holy in all the borders thereof round about."

Nathan is implying that the land is completely flat (straight) so that it won't fit properly on a curved earth, but only on a flat earth; which is a ridiculous premise. Nathan is making a false association, as an area of land that is very long and wide doesn't mean that the land is completely flat.

It's illogical for Nathan to declare that this verse is saying that the earth is flat, with no curvature. This is what he and other flat-earthers do, they press their beliefs upon Scripture, to make it seem like it's proclaiming that the earth is flat. Flat-earthers, how do you defend Ezekiel 45:1 being on the list?

"That he would grant you, according to the riches of his glory, to be strengthened with might by his Spirit in the inner man; That Christ may dwell in your hearts by faith; that ye, being rooted and grounded in love, May be able to comprehend with all saints what is the breadth, and length, and depth, and height. And to know the love of Christ, which passeth knowledge, that ye might be filled with all the fullness of God."
Ephesians 3:16-19

CHAPTER 14

A "PLAIN" can't exist on a ball, only a "FLAT/LEVEL" surface, of which, Yeshua (aka Jesus) stood upon.

Nathan cites Luke 6:17 *"And he came down with them, and stood in the plain, and the company of his disciples, and a great multitude of people out of all Judaea and Jerusalem, and from the sea coast of Tyre and Sidon, which came to hear him, and to be healed of their diseases."*

The fact that the verse declares that Messiah *"came down"* tells you that it's not declaring that the earth is flat. When you read the context, you see that five verses earlier, in Luke 6:12, it tells us that they went *"up"* to a mountain to pray. *"And it came to pass in those days, that he went out into a mountain to pray, and continued all night in prayer to God."*

Luke 6:17 is saying that they *came down* the mountain. It's amazing how desperate Nathan is to find verses which supposedly proclaim that the earth is flat, but we can see that he's misrepresenting the context. He's pushing his belief onto the text, to proclaim that a plain can't exist on a globe earth.

How is this verse even on a flat-earth proof list? And how do people promote this list? Is it because they blindly trust Nathan?

I hope that you see a trend with Nathan's explanations. When I read through his verse list; I was appalled. He either has a major lack of understanding of the context of Scripture, or he's blatantly disregarding it. And sadly, it gets much worse in the next chapter.

CHAPTER 15

Paths are Straight, not curved

Nathan cites 1 Samuel 6:12, Psalm 5:8, Psalm 27:11, Isaiah 40:3, Jeremiah 31:9, Matthew 3:3, Mark 1:3, Luke 3:4, John 1:23, Acts 16:11, Acts 21:1, Hebrews 12:13

Nathan is proclaiming that *all paths are straight* and that these verses prove that the earth is flat. What kind of logic is this? Do we think that Scripture is proclaiming that all paths are straight?

These verses metaphorically point to crook paths, which invalidates that all paths are straight. Isaiah 59:8 says that there are crooked paths, *"The way of peace they know not; and there is no judgment in their goings: they have made them crooked paths: whosoever goeth therein shall not know peace."* So does Lamentations 3:9: *"He hath inclosed my ways with hewn stone, he hath made my paths crooked."*

Read the verses that Nathan cites and ask yourself; is it referring to a real path on the earth, or is it a metaphor?

1 Samuel 6:12 *"And the kine took the straight way to the way of Bethshemesh, and went along the highway, lowing as they went, and turned not aside to the right hand or to the left; and the lords of the Philistines went after them unto the border of Bethshemesh."*

It's simply saying that they took the most direct course.

Psalms 5:8 *"Lead me, O LORD, in thy righteousness because of mine enemies; make thy way straight before my face."*

It's not talking about a straight, physical path. David is asking Yahuah to cause him to walk a path of righteousness, to lead him out of the dangers of his enemies. It's an abomination to include this as a flat earth verse!

Psalms 27:11 *"Teach me thy way, O LORD, and lead me in a plain path, because of mine enemies."*

Nathan says this is a great verse about walking a straight path of obedience, as well as another Biblical proof that we're living on a flat earth. He asks, *"if the earth isn't flat, how are we to understand and identify with walking a straight path?"*

Seriously? Did he not try to walk a *straight path* of obeying the commands of Scripture, before he believed that the earth is flat? We could live on a figure-eight shaped earth, and walking a *straight path* means following Yahuah's instructions for our lives!

Nathan says that if God created the globe earth, then the verse should ask the Lord to *"lead me in a curved path."*

Statements like that make my jaw drop! He says that many other verses would be invalid if the earth is a globe because they teach about paths that should be straight.

I can't even comprehend that Nathan says these things, as they're so absurd! Verses about walking a straight path, which means to strive to live a righteous life before our Heavenly Father, have absolutely nothing to do with the shape of the earth!

Isaiah 40:3 *"The voice of him that crieth in the wilderness, Prepare ye the way of the LORD, make straight in the desert a highway for our God."*

Do we believe that this verse is telling them to make a straight line in the desert? It's foretelling John the Baptist, who preached repentance to the Jews, preparing the way for our Messiah.

Isaiah 40:4 continues the prophetic vision about John the Baptist, *"Every valley shall be exalted, and every mountain and hill shall be made low: and the crooked shall be made straight, and the rough places plain."*

Luke 3:3-6 proclaims that Isaiah spoke about John the Baptist. *"And he came into all the country about Jordan, preaching the baptism of repentance for the remission of sins; As it is written in the book of the words of Isaiah the prophet, saying, The voice of one crying in the wilderness, Prepare ye the way of the Lord, make his paths straight. Every valley shall be filled, and every mountain and hill shall be brought low; and the crooked shall be made straight, and the rough ways shall be made smooth; And all flesh shall see the salvation of God."*

Citing Isaiah 40:3 as a flat earth verse is a pathetic perversion of Scripture by Nathan.

Jeremiah 31:9 *"They shall come with weeping, and with supplications will I lead them: I will cause them to walk by the rivers of waters in a straight way, wherein they shall not stumble: for I am a father to Israel, and Ephraim is my firstborn."*

It's simply saying that Yahuah will lead them down a straight path of obedience; it's not describing the shape of the earth. How in the world do Nathan and other flat-earthers proclaim that this is a flat earth verse?

Matthew 3:3 *"For this is he that was spoken of by the prophet Esaias, saying, The voice of one crying in the wilderness, Prepare ye the way of the Lord, make his paths straight."*

Mark 1:3 *"The voice of one crying in the wilderness, Prepare ye the way of the Lord, make his paths straight."*

Luke 3:4 *"As it is written in the book of the words of Esaias the prophet, saying, The voice of one crying in the wilderness, Prepare ye the way of the Lord, make his paths straight."*

John 1:23 *"He said, I am the voice of one crying in the wilderness, Make straight the way of the Lord, as said the prophet Esaias."*

These verses, which are obviously about John the Baptist *preparing the way* for Messiah; *making His path straight* by preaching repentance; have been taken out of context by Nathan, to proclaim that they say that the earth is flat. I can't comprehend the mindset which causes someone to do such a thing!

Acts 16:11 *"Therefore loosing from Troas, we came with a straight course to Samothracia, and the next day to Neapolis;"*

It's simply saying that they sailed directly to Samothracia, stayed the night, and then the next day they set sail for Neapolis.

Acts 21:1 *"And it came to pass, that after we were gotten from them, and had launched, we came with a straight course unto Coos, and the day following unto Rhodes, and from thence unto Patara."*

It's saying that they sailed directly to Coos, stayed the night, and then the next day they set sail for Rhodes. Do you see how the mindset of flat-earthers causes them not to be able to comprehend what Scripture is describing or to blatantly disregard it?

These explanations are so bad that it seems like a fifth-grader was asked to find flat earth Bible verses, and they grabbed any verse which seems to point to a straight path.

Hebrews 12:13 *"And make straight paths for your feet, lest that which is lame be turned out of the way; but let it rather be healed."*

It's telling us to keep the right course, to follow Messiah's instructions, to be a good example for others. How in the world is this a flat earth verse?

Nathan cites these verses so that he can claim that there are hundreds of verses which proclaim that the Earth is flat, but we can see that he's taking them out of context. This is a clear abuse of Scripture by someone whose mind is skewed by flat-earth zealotry.

Explanations like these are what compelled me to write this book, to debunk Nathan's verse list because he should know better than to proclaim that these verses are pointing to a flat earth. And I'm appalled at seeing people promote these verses.

The irony is that if you travel east or west on the flat earth, your path is not *straight*, as east and west *curve* around the North Pole. But on the globe earth, you can continuously travel east and west, neither veering to the left nor the right.

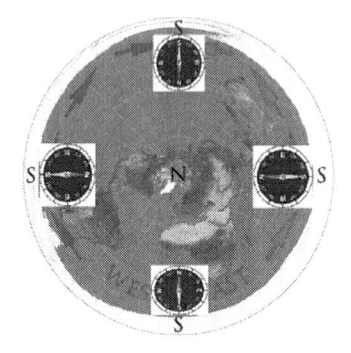

If you're a flat-earther, how do you justify the five verses which are about John the Baptist preparing the way for Messiah; being on the flat earth verse list? How do you justify verses about our need to walk a straight path of obedience before our Heavenly Father, being on the flat earth verse list?

How do you proclaim to people that the Bible describes a flat earth when you see how badly they're taken out of context? And why are you not confronting Nathan Roberts about these explanations?

"The way of the just is uprightness: thou, most upright, dost weigh the path of the just."
Isaiah 26:7

CHAPTER 16

Waters are Straight, not curved

Nathan cites Job 37:10 *"By the breath of God frost is given: and the breadth of the waters is straitened."*

About this verse, Nathan proclaims, *"if that doesn't settle it once and for all, I don't know what will."*

It's interesting that Nathan thinks that this is a slam-dunk flat earth proof because the verse says that the waters are *"straitened,"* which means that the water wasn't straight beforehand. The context of Job 37 is the weather; including the words *lightning, thunder, snow, rain, cold* and *thick clouds*. The previous verse describes cold winds coming out of the north, *"Out of the south cometh the whirlwind: and cold out of the north."*

The Strong's Hebrew word for *"frost"* is 7140 *qerach;* which means *ice; hence, hail; by resemblance, rock crystal:—crystal, frost, ice.*

Job's proclaiming that by Yahuah's breath, by the cold air out of the north, the waters become solid ice, so that they become *"straitened."* When a lake freezes over, the waters on top are not able to move.

The English Standard Version says, *"By the breath of God ice is given, and the broad waters are frozen fast."* The Berean Study Bible says, *"By the breath of God the ice is formed and the watery expanses are frozen."* The New American Standard 1977 says, *"From the breath of God ice is made, and the expanse of the waters is frozen."*

Whenever you see a lake that's frozen, you see water that's been *straightened*. Because Nathan believes that all water is flat, he forces that belief onto Scripture to take this verse out of context. Flat-earthers, how do you defend Job 37:10 being on the list?

CHAPTER 17

Earthquakes shake Earth and does not move

Nathan cites 2 Samuel 22:8, Isaiah 13:13, Revelation 6:12-13

The fact that an earthquake doesn't move the earth out of its place in the universe does not prove that it's flat.

2 Samuel 22:8 *"Then the earth shook and trembled; the foundations of heaven moved and shook because he was wroth."*

It's using poetic language, as the context of the verse is the deliverance of his servant and the destruction of his enemies. Read the seven verses before it, and you see all of the symbolic language, and the proper context.

"And David spake unto the LORD the words of this song in the day that the LORD had delivered him out of the hand of all his enemies, and out of the hand of Saul: And he said, The LORD is my rock, and my fortress, and my deliverer; The God of my rock; in him will I trust: he is my shield, and the horn of my salvation, my high tower, and my refuge, my saviour; thou savest me from violence. I will call on the LORD, who is worthy to be praised: so shall I be saved from mine enemies. When the waves of death compassed me, the floods of ungodly men made me afraid; The sorrows of hell compassed me about; the snares of death prevented me; In my distress I called upon the LORD, and cried to my God: and he did hear my voice out of his temple, and my cry did enter into his ears." HalleluYah!

Isaiah 13:13 *"Therefore I will shake the heavens, and the earth shall remove out of her place, in the wrath of the LORD of hosts, and in the day of his fierce anger."*

The earth being moved out of its place can point to a geocentric earth, as it's normally fixed. But the context of the verse is not talking about the physical earth.

It's using symbolic language to convey commotions and judgment. Isaiah 13:17 tells us that it's pointing to the political upheaval of the Medes being sent by Yahuah to attack the Babylonians: *"Behold, I will stir up the Medes against them, which shall not regard silver; and as for gold, they shall not delight in it."*

Revelation 6:12-13 *"And I beheld when he had opened the sixth seal, and, lo, there was a great earthquake; and the sun became black as sackcloth of hair, and the moon became as blood; And the stars of heaven fell unto the earth, even as a fig tree casteth her untimely figs, when she is shaken of a mighty wind."*

This is a prophetic passage that uses symbolism to describe great upheaval. Many people point to the sixth seal as an end-time event, as the sun has been darkened; so in that case, it's not describing a normal situation on earth. And it doesn't say whether the earth is moved or not, so it doesn't confirm Nathan's point. Since Nathan's claim about *earthquakes* is without merit, let's focus on some real earthquakes that changed the whole earth!

"Jesus, when he had cried again with a loud voice, yielded up the ghost. And, behold, the veil of the temple was rent in twain from the top to the bottom; and the earth did quake, and the rocks rent; And the graves were opened; and many bodies of the saints which slept arose, And came out of the graves after his resurrection, and went into the holy city, and appeared unto many. Now when the centurion, and they that were with him, watching Jesus, saw the earthquake, and those things that were done, they feared greatly, saying, Truly this was the Son of God." Matthew 27:50-54

"And, behold, there was a great earthquake: for the angel of the Lord descended from heaven, and came and rolled back the stone from the door, and sat upon it. And the angel answered and said unto the women, Fear not ye: for I know that ye seek Jesus, which was crucified. He is not here: for he is risen, as he said. Come, see the place where the Lord lay." Matthew 28:2, 5-6 HalleluYah!

CHAPTER 18

Earth is fixed and immovable

Nathan cites 1 Chronicles 16:30, Psalm 33:9, Psalm 93:1, Psalm 96:10, Psalm 104:5, Psalm 119:89-90, Isaiah 14:7, Isaiah 45:18, Zechariah 1:11, Hebrews 11:10, 2 Peter 3:5

A geocentric earth is fixed at the center of the universe and immovable, so these verses don't prove that the earth is flat. You'll see that some of his explanations are based on him taking verses literally instead of understanding that they're using a metaphor. Here are some examples of metaphorical verses which say that the earth is moved.

Psalms 99:1 is pointing to a time when Messiah's return will cause his enemies to have reason to tremble. *"The LORD reigneth; let the people tremble: he sitteth between the cherubims; let the earth be moved."*

Jeremiah 50:46 symbolizes the fall of Babylon. *"At the noise of the taking of Babylon the earth is moved, and the cry is heard among the nations."*

Read through Nathan's list and ask yourself, is this verse about the physical earth, or is it using a metaphor?

1 Chronicles 16:30 *"Fear before him, all the earth: the world also shall be stable, that it be not moved."*

The context of the next verse is not the physical earth rejoicing, but rather it's using symbolic language. *"Let the heavens be glad, and let the earth rejoice: and let men say among the nations, The LORD reigneth."*

It's telling us to humble ourselves before the Heavenly Father, whose creation is under His mighty hand. It's not making a statement about the earth being fixed in place. It's declaring that the kingdom of Yahuah shall never be moved.

Psalms 33:9 *"For he spake, and it was (done); he commanded, and it stood fast."*

What's the context? Psalms 33:6-8 says, *"By the word of the LORD were the heavens made; and all the host of them by the breath of his mouth. He gathereth the waters of the sea together as an heap: he layeth up the depth in storehouses. Let all the earth fear the LORD: let all the inhabitants of the world stand in awe of him."*

A geocentric globe earth also stands fast in the middle of the universe, so this verse doesn't prove that the earth is flat. It's telling us to be in awe of our Creator, who spoke the earth and universe into existence, which obeyed His commands during creation.

Psalms 93:1 *"The LORD reigneth, he is clothed with majesty; the LORD is clothed with strength, wherewith he hath girded himself: the world also is established, that it cannot be moved."*

The context is pointing to Yahuah's government of this world, His leaders, which cannot be moved; so it's not talking about the physical earth. The next verse says, *"Thy throne is established of old: thou art from everlasting."*

The kingdom of Yahuah is established and everlasting, *"And in the days of these kings shall the God of heaven set up a kingdom, which shall never be destroyed: and the kingdom shall not be left to other people, but it shall break in pieces and consume all these kingdoms, and it shall stand for ever."* Daniel 2:44

Psalms 96:10 *"Say among the heathen that the LORD reigneth: the world also shall be established that it shall not be moved: he shall judge the people righteously."*

Read Psalms 96. Does it have anything to do with the creation of the earth or the design of the earth? No, it's a Psalm of David, a prophecy of the coming of the Messiah, and of the calling of the Gentiles to believe in Him.

The next verse symbolically talks about the earth being glad, *"Let the heavens rejoice, and let the earth be glad; let the sea roar, and the fulness thereof."* Psalms 96:11

It's saying that the kingdom of Yahuah, which is made up of those who have a covenant relationship with Him through the Son, will not be moved; and that they will rejoice at His righteous judgments.

Psalms 104:5 *"Who laid the foundations of the earth, that it should not be removed for ever."*

The Hebrew word for *foundations* is 4349 *makown*; which means *properly, a fixture, i.e., a basis; generally a place, especially as an abode: foundation, habitation, (dwelling-, settled) place.*

It's not pointing to the earth being moved in space; rather it's talking about the foundation of the earth itself. Though it may be shaken by earthquakes, the structure of the earth will hold true.

There's no proof of what the *"foundations"* of the flat earth are made of or how it's designed; but we can see how the globe earth has five different layers, foundations, each which serve a purpose to make the planet stable. There's an inner core, an outer core, a mantle, an upper mantle, and the crust upon which the oceans and continents set.

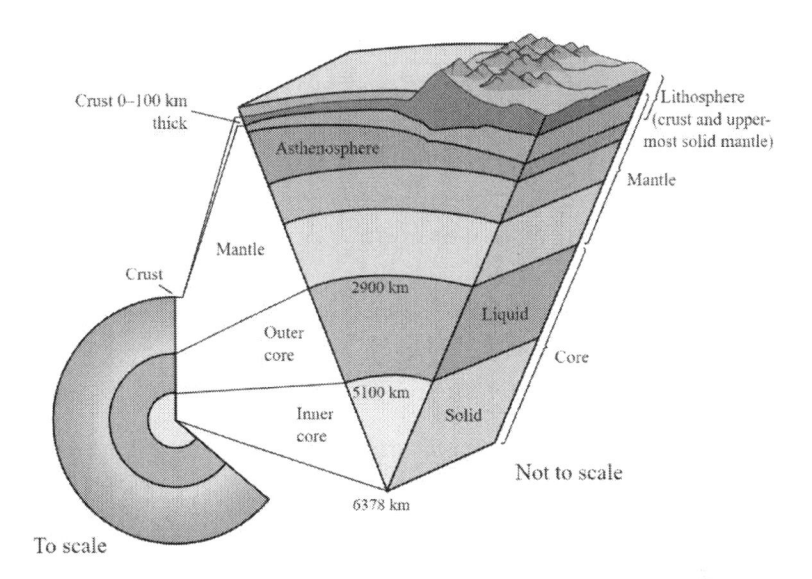

[Diagram: Cross-section of the earth showing Crust 0-100 km thick, Lithosphere (crust and uppermost solid mantle), Asthenosphere, Mantle, Outer core (Liquid) at 2900 km, Inner core (Solid) at 5100 km, 6378 km total. Labels: "To scale" and "Not to scale".]

Nathan refers to this image of the core layers of the globe earth, and asked, *"How do we know that these are the actual layers of the earth? Who went there to verify? How was it accomplished, and when?"*

Nathan is claiming that we have to see it in person or it's not real. That's ironic because flat-earthers have never seen the supposed glass dome or the end of the flat earth, but they believe in it. And flat-earthers have no proof of what material makes up the layers below the surface of a flat earth, or how far down it goes.

We have the technology to be able to understand what materials make up the different layers of the globe earth and to know their thickness, so nobody needs to drill down that far or go there to verify it.

Psalms 119:89-90 *"For ever, O LORD, thy word is settled in heaven. Thy faithfulness is unto all generations: thou hast established the earth, and it abideth."*

Nathan is proclaiming that the flat earth abideth, that it stands still.

This proves the heliocentric globe earth theory is wrong, but a geocentric globe earth does that too, so it's not a flat earth proof.

It's proclaiming that just as the earth is stable and has not been removed since creation, so too is Yahuah's *faithfulness*, which has endured through all of the generations of men who have lived on the earth.

Psalms 89:1 says, *"I will sing of the mercies of the LORD for ever: with my mouth will I make known thy faithfulness to all generations."*

Isaiah 14:7 *"The whole earth is at rest, and is quiet: they break forth into singing."*

This verse isn't about the physical earth. Isaiah 14:1-3 says, *"For the LORD will have mercy on Jacob, and will yet choose Israel, and set them in their own land: and the strangers shall be joined with them, and they shall cleave to the house of Jacob. And the people shall take them, and bring them to their place: and the house of Israel shall possess them in the land of the LORD for servants and handmaids: and they shall take them captives, whose captives they were; and they shall rule over their oppressors. And it shall come to pass in the day that the LORD shall give thee rest from thy sorrow, and from thy fear, and from the hard bondage wherein thou wast made to serve."*

It's talking about the *peace* that came after the fall of the kingdom of Babylon, which had oppressed many on *earth*, including the Jews who had been taken captive by the Babylonians. The Medo-Persian Empire was sent to conquer Babylon, which led to the Jews being released from captivity and empowered to rebuild the city of Jerusalem and the temple. Did they break forth in song during these events? Yes!

Once again, Nathan has cited a verse that's not talking about the physical properties of the earth, to proclaim it as a flat earth verse.

Isaiah 45:18 *"For thus saith the LORD that created the heavens; God himself that formed the earth and made it; he hath established it, he created it not in vain, he formed it to be inhabited: I am the LORD, and there is none else."*

Though this verse is about the creation of the heavens and the earth, it only states the Yahuah formed the earth and established it, which doesn't prove that it's flat.

Zechariah 1:11 *"And they answered the angel of the LORD that stood among the myrtle trees, and said, We have walked to and fro through the earth, and, behold, all the earth sitteth still, and is at rest."*

It's using symbolic language to describe a time of general peace, when the earth was free from wars, as it was in the second year of the reign of Darius of the Persian Empire. Wars were suspended at that time, though they would soon break out again.

Once again, Nathan has cited a verse that's not talking about the physical properties of the earth; so it's not a flat earth verse. And even it if was talking about the physical earth, a geocentric earth sits still too.

Hebrews 11:10 *"For he looked for a city which hath foundations, whose builder and maker is God."*

Where does this verse say that the earth is fixed and immovable? It's talking about the city of Jerusalem, not the whole earth. And it's not even talking about physical Jerusalem, but to heavenly Jerusalem, as declared in Hebrews 12:22, *"But ye are come unto mount Sion, and unto the city of the living God, the heavenly Jerusalem, and to an innumerable company of angels,"*

Abraham understood that true Jerusalem is not made by men, but by Yahuah, and its citizens are the set-apart saints.

2 Peter 3:5 *"For this they willingly are ignorant of, that by the word of God the heavens were of old, and the earth standing out of the water and in the water."*

I'm not sure how Nathan thinks that this verse proves that the earth is fixed and immovable, as it doesn't say anything like that. It's pointing to people who mock the saints about Messiah's promise to come in power and glory, *"Knowing this first, that there shall come in the last days scoffers, walking after their own lusts, And saying, Where is the promise of his coming? for since the fathers fell asleep, all things continue as they were from the beginning of the creation."* 2 Peter 3:3-4

Peter compares them to those who mocked Noah, saying, *"where's the rain?"* Before the flood, it didn't rain on the earth, as mist watered the earth. And when the rain came, the land was covered by water, and the mockers were swept away by the water.

2 Peter 3:6-10 says, *"Whereby the world that then was, being overflowed with water, perished: But the heavens and the earth, which are now, by the same word are kept in store, reserved unto fire against the day of judgment and perdition of ungodly men. But the day of the Lord will come as a thief in the night; in which the heavens shall pass away with a great noise, and the elements shall melt with fervent heat, the earth also and the works that are therein shall be burned up."*

Peter is saying that just as people mocked Noah, people mock the saints, saying where is your Messiah who promised to return?

Those unprepared for Messiah *coming in the clouds of judgment* will be caught off-guard, just as the people were caught by surprise when the rains came and flooded the earth. For them, it will be a day of judgment of fire, instead of water.

In Nathan's explanation about these verses in his book, he cites the *Michelson-Morley Experiment*, saying that it confirms that the earth is motionless. The hypocrisy of Nathan citing that experiment is that it's based on the globe earth, not a flat earth!

Do you see how he operates? He cites an experiment to proclaim that it points to a still earth, to promote his flat earth beliefs; but he neglects to tell you that it's based on scientific experiments of the globe earth. That's intellectual dishonesty!

The experiment was set up to prove that the earth is heliocentric, but it did the opposite. It found that the Earth is standing still in space, which provided astounding and devastating evidence to destroy the Copernican Principle. Albert Michelson reluctantly said, *"This conclusion directly contradicts the explanation… which presupposes that the Earth moves."*

Nathan also references an experiment that's dubbed with the name *Airy's Failure*. George Bidell Airy conducted an experiment to prove heliocentrism, but the result of the experiment indicated that Earth is stationary, so it didn't prove that the earth is moving and is called *Airy's Failure*.

Again, the hypocrisy of Nathan citing the *Airy's Failure* experiment is that it's based on a globe earth; not a flat earth. The irony is that by citing those studies, it means that Nathan is ignorantly providing proof that the earth is a geocentric globe!

Flat-earthers, how do you defend these verses being on the list?

"Therefore, my beloved brethren, be ye steadfast, unmovable, always abounding in the work of the Lord, forasmuch as ye know that your labor is not in vain in the Lord."
1 Corinthians 15:58

CHAPTER 19

"Be still, and know that I am God."

Nathan cites Psalms 46:10 *"Be still, and know that I am God: I will be exalted among the heathen, I will be exalted in the earth."*

He says that he was perplexed about how he could *"be still"* if the earth is spinning and flying through space; but now that he believes that the earth is flat, it makes sense that he needs to stop moving.

That explanation makes my head *spin*. No matter what the shape of the earth is, the concept is very straight-forward; amid trouble, we need not fear, for Yahuah is our strength and our refuge. Flat-earthers, how do you defend Psalms 46:10 being on the list?

It's getting crazy in these end times, so let's read the whole chapter, to reinforce that our Heavenly Father is in control and that He's our refuge in times of need.

"God is our refuge and strength, a very present help in trouble. Therefore will not we fear, though the earth be removed, and though the mountains be carried into the midst of the sea; Though the waters thereof roar and be troubled, though the mountains shake with the swelling thereof. Selah. There is a river, the streams whereof shall make glad the city of God, the holy place of the tabernacles of the most High. God is in the midst of her; she shall not be moved: God shall help her, and that right early. The heathen raged, the kingdoms were moved: he uttered his voice, the earth melted. The LORD of hosts is with us; the God of Jacob is our refuge. Selah. Come, behold the works of the LORD, what desolations he hath made in the earth. He maketh wars to cease unto the end of the earth; he breaketh the bow, and cutteth the spear in sunder; he burneth the chariot in the fire. Be still, and know that I am God: I will be exalted among the heathen, I will be exalted in the earth. The LORD of hosts is with us; the God of Jacob is our refuge. Selah" HalleluYah!

CHAPTER 20

Earth has Pillars and hangs on nothing

Nathan cites 1 Samuel 2:8, Job 9:6, Job 26:7, Psalm 75:3

Nathan is saying that the pillars in these verses are literal pillars which are under the flat earth.

First, let's apply logic. In the design of a building, where are pillars placed? On a firm foundation, so that they can support the structure that's above them. Does it make any sense to place pillars under the flat earth, since the pillars would not be mounted on top anything solid? No!

Rob Skiba shows a drawing of the flat earth like this, which has water above the glass dome and below the flat earth. This means that the pillars below the flat earth are set upon the water, which is nonsensical.

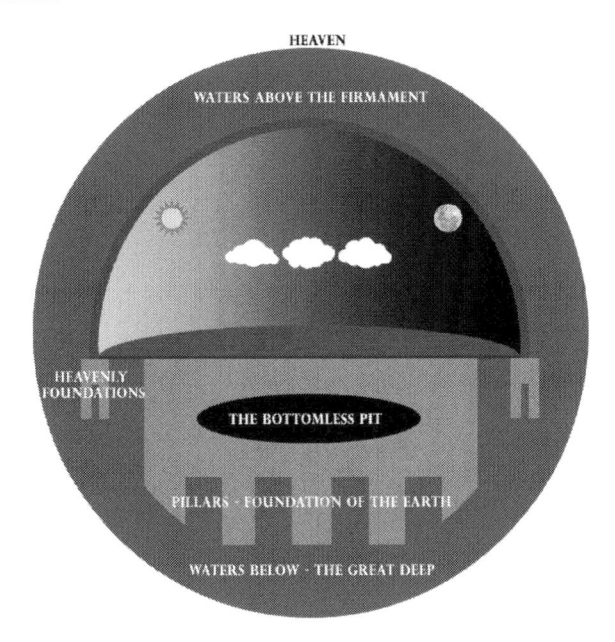

Rob made a conceptualized design which he calls *YHWH's Terrarium*. It's ironic that flat-earthers reject pictures of the globe earth, saying that they're CGI; but they don't have any pictures, only CGI models.

Rob cites Job 38:6 to point to the *foundations* of the flat earth, *"Whereupon are the foundations thereof fastened? or who laid the corner stone thereof."* He points out that our Creator is speaking *of "laying a foundation"* with a *"corner stone"* that is *"fastened"* in place.

Rob says, *"If ever there was a Flat-earther, anti-globalist Scripture, this one is it. How do you twist and distort that Scripture to fit a rotating globe, freely floating in space? Where is the "fastened foundation" with a "corner stone" in that model?"*

A cornerstone is placed to sustain the principal weight of an edifice. Where would a cornerstone be placed on the flat earth model to sustain the weight of it? Would the cornerstone be placed on open space? On water? You can see that Rob's argument has no merit.

Job wasn't describing a literal *"stone"* on the corner of the earth but was pointing to the foundation of the earth. A globe earth with foundations of different materials which make up its core makes more sense.

It's ironic that Nathan posted a video about the pillars that are under the domed arch entrance of Brenau University. He proclaims that's how the flat earth is set up, with pillars underneath to support it, but ignores that the pillars are set on a solid foundation.

1 Samuel 2:8 *"He raiseth up the poor out of the dust, and lifteth up the beggar from the dunghill, to set them among princes, and to make them inherit the throne of glory: for the pillars of the earth are the LORD'S, and he hath set the world upon them."*

The word *"pillars"* in 1 Samuel 2:8 is not talking about physical pillars. If someone says that a person is a *'pillar in the community,'* it means that they're a *supportive leader*. Figuratively, *the pillars of the earth* may design the princes of the world, the supreme rulers of it, and civil magistrates; those who Yahuah uses for His purposes.

The previous verse is talking about lifting people up and making them rich; so we can see that the context is about people, not physical pillars. *"The LORD maketh poor, and maketh rich: he bringeth low, and lifteth up."* 1 Samuel 2:7

Galatians 2:9 shows that leaders in the early church are symbolized as *pillars*. *"And when James, Cephas, and John, <u>who seemed to be pillars</u>, perceived the grace that was given unto me, they gave to me and Barnabas the right hands of fellowship; that we should go unto the heathen, and they unto the circumcision."*

Revelation 3:12 describes the leaders of Messiah's kingdom as pillars. *"Him that overcometh will I make a pillar in the temple of my God, and he shall go no more out: and I will write upon him the name of my God, and the name of the city of my God, which is new Jerusalem, which cometh down out of heaven from my God: and I will write upon him my new name."*

Are they physical temple pillars? No, they're leaders in Messiah's assembly of saints. 1 Samuel 2:8 isn't a flat earth proof, as it's not about physical pillars.

Job 9:6 *"Which shaketh the earth out of her place, and the pillars thereof tremble."*

Oddly, Nathan points to verses to proclaim that the earth is immovable, but then he cites a verse that says that the earth is shaken out of its place.

If the earth is shaken out of its place, would the leaders (*pillars*) of the earth tremble? If there's a violent commotion, would the leaders (*pillars*) of the earth not tremble? If the literal earth is shaken out of its place, the supports of the flat earth or globe earth will tremble, so there's no way to proclaim that it's a flat earth verse.

Job 26:7 *"He stretcheth out the north over the empty place, and hangeth the earth upon nothing."*

Nathan proclaims that the flat earth is supported by *pillars*, which is why the earth is not suspended from anything. Daniel Valles in his *Circle of the Earth Investigation*, says, *"The earth is not hanging or suspended over nothingness (space); the Bible makes it clear that foundations and pillars are supporting the earth. There isn't anything that the world is hanging from - it is set upon."*

A flat earth which is supported by pillars under it negates the point that Job is making, that the earth is hung upon nothing.

If a statue of King David is mounted on a pillar, do we proclaim that's its hung up nothing? No!

The Hebrew word for *hangs* is 8518 *talah*; which means *to suspend, to hang (up)*.

In the twenty-six other verses where the word *talah* is used, they all refer to something that is suspended from above, such as people who have been hanged; and none of them point to the object being supported by something below.

Ironically, we have pictures of the globe earth which prove that it hangs on *nothing*; but we don't have pictures of the flat earth to prove it. We'll discuss this verse in much more detail in another chapter, as Nathan mentions it again.

Psalms 75:3 *"The earth and all the inhabitants thereof are dissolved: I bear up the pillars of it. Selah."*

It's talking about people, the inhabitants, the righteous; who will be preserved, though the earth (*erets*, land, country) is laid waste. Once again, the word *pillars* is pointing to leaders. Psalms 75:10 describes the wicked being cut off from leadership, as a *"horn"* symbolizes a leader. *"All the horns of the wicked also will I cut off; but the horns of the righteous shall be exalted."*

Yahuah supports and establishes a nation with His set-apart people, His *pillars*, who uphold His laws and provide justice to the people. Flat-earthers, these verses have not proven that the earth is flat, how do you defend them being on the list?

"It is God that girdeth me with strength, and maketh my way perfect. He maketh my feet like hinds' feet, and setteth me upon my high places."
Psalms 18:32-33

CHAPTER 21

Earth has a Face (a geometrical flat surface)

Nathan cites Genesis 1:29, Genesis 4:14, Genesis 6:1, Genesis 6:7, Genesis 7:3, Genesis 7:4, Genesis 8:9, Genesis 11:8, Genesis 11:9, Genesis 41:56, Exodus 32:12, Exodus 33:16, Numbers 12:3, Deuteronomy 6:15, Deuteronomy 7:6, 1 Samuel 20:15, 1 Kings 13:34, Job 37:12, Psalm 104:30, Jeremiah 25:26, Jeremiah 28:16, Ezekiel 34:6, Ezekiel 38:20, Ezekiel 39:14, Amos 9:6, Amos 9:8, Zechariah 5:3, Luke 12:56, Luke 21:35

Nathan says that the word *"face"* has no application to a globe earth, asking, *"where would be the front/face of the earth?"* He asks which part of a ball is the face?

In the movie *Cast Away*, Chuck Noland (Tom Hanks) knows which side of a volleyball has a face.

The Hebrew word for *"face"* in Genesis 1:29 is 6440 *paniym; the face (as the part that turns); used in a great variety of applications (literally and figuratively), 1,890 times used in a great variety of applications (literally and figuratively); also (with prepositional prefix) as a preposition (before, etc.):— accept, a-(be-)fore(-time), against, anger, as (long as),*

battle, because (of), beseech, countenance, edge, employ, endure, enquire, face, favour, fear of, for, forefront(-part), form(-er time, -ward), from, front, heaviness, him(-self), honourable, impudent, in, it, look(-eth) (- s), me, meet, more than, mouth, of, off, (of) old (time), on, open, out of, over against, the partial, person, please, presence, propect, was purposed, by reason of, regard, right forth, serve, shewbread, sight, state, straight, street, thee, them(-selves), through (+ - out), till, time(-s) past, (un-)to(-ward), upon, upside (+ down), with(- in, + -stand), ye, you.

Do any of those words proclaim that the word *"face"* is a *geometric flat surface*? No, that's just Nathan's biased interpretation.

Ironically, in the section of his book about the moon, Nathan makes statements to try to disprove that the moon is on an axis; and he points out that *"the same portion of the moon is always facing you."* He's saying that the *face* of the moon is the side that's towards us, so he's proclaiming that a globe-shaped object has a *face*, but he doesn't understand how a globe earth has a face. That's amazing!

Webster's 1828 Dictionary defines *face*: *In a general sense, the surface of a thing, or the side which presents itself to the view of a spectator; as the face of the earth; the face of the waters.*

That definition refutes Nathan's assertion that a globe doesn't have a face, and Scripture does not say that the earth has a geometrical flat surface.

Daniel Valles, in his *Circle of the Earth Investigation* book, says, "The Bible states that Earth has a Face - not a Surface. The Bible always refers to the "face of the earth" (29 times!) In solid geometry, a face is a flat (planar) surface that forms part of the boundary of a solid object." He's saying that the earth has a face, not a *'surface;'* but then in his definition, he says that a face is a surface. Daniel continues, "A sphere is a closed surface there is no boundary, and it's not flat or planar."

Does a volleyball have a surface? Yes! Daniel's reasoning sounds like *circular* logic to me.

Read through the verses that Nathan listed and you'll see that none of them are describing the shape of the earth. It's tedious to look at the proper context of each verse, but it shows you how Nathan is abusing the Scriptures.

Genesis 1:29 *"And God said, Behold, I have given you every herb bearing seed, which is upon the face of all the earth, and every tree, in the which is the fruit of a tree yielding seed; to you it shall be for meat."*

The word *"earth"* is the Hebrew word *erets*, which isn't pointing to the whole earth; but to the *land*, the *ground*. Genesis 1:29 is pointing to herbs and trees growing on the land.

Genesis 4:14 *"Behold, thou hast driven me out this day from the face of the earth; and from thy face shall I be hid; and I shall be a fugitive and a vagabond in the earth; and it shall come to pass, that every one that findeth me shall slay me."*

Cain was forced to leave the *land* that he grew up in, where his family lived; as he was banished to a strange place at a distance from all that he was familiar with, as a punishment to him.

Genesis 6:1 *"And it came to pass, when men began to multiply on the face of the earth, and daughters were born unto them,"*

People live on the *land*, on the *ground* of the earth.

Genesis 6:7 *"And the LORD said, I will destroy man whom I have created from the face of the earth; both man, and beast, and the creeping thing, and the fowls of the air; for it repenteth me that I have made them."*

It's saying that the *land* will be flooded so that they're destroyed.

Genesis 7:3 *"Of fowls also of the air by sevens, the male and the female; to keep seed alive upon the face of all the earth."*

Birds spread seed around the *ground,* causing vegetation to grow.

Genesis 7:4 *"For yet seven days, and I will cause it to rain upon the earth forty days and forty nights; and every living substance that I have made will I destroy from off the face of the earth."*

The *land* was flooded so that every living thing was destroyed.

Genesis 8:9 *"But the dove found no rest for the sole of her foot, and she returned unto him into the ark, for the waters were on the face of the whole earth: then he put forth his hand, and took her, and pulled her in unto him into the ark."*

The floodwaters covered all of the *land* on the earth.

Genesis 11:8 *"So the LORD scattered them abroad from thence upon the face of all the earth: and they left off to build the city."*

Men were scattered from Babylon across the *land* of the earth.

Genesis 11:9 *"Therefore is the name of it called Babel; because the LORD did there confound the language of all the earth: and from thence did the LORD scatter them abroad upon the face of all the earth."*

Men were scattered across the *land* of the earth to separate them.

Genesis 41:56 *"And the famine was over all the face of the earth: And Joseph opened all the storehouses, and sold unto the Egyptians; and the famine waxed sore in the land of Egypt."*

It's describing famine in the *land* of Egypt.

Exodus 32:12 *"Wherefore should the Egyptians speak, and say, For mischief did he bring them out, to slay them in the mountains, and to consume them from the face of the earth? Turn from thy fierce wrath, and repent of this evil against thy people."*

After the Israelites made a golden calf while Moses was up on the mountain, Yahuah was going to smite them all and make a great nation from Moses. Moses pleaded with Yahuah, pointing out that the Egyptians would mock Him if He caused these people to come out of Egypt by miracles, only to smite them Himself. So the context is that Yahuah was going to smite the Israelites who were in the *land* near Mount Sinai.

Exodus 33:16 *"For wherein shall it be known here that I and thy people have found grace in thy sight? is it not in that thou goest with us? so shall we be separated, I and thy people, from all the people that are upon the face of the earth."*

It's saying that the Israelites were a distinguished people, set-apart from the other people groups of the world, who were given the promised *land*.

Numbers 12:3 *"Now the man Moses was very meek, above all the men which were upon the face of the earth."*

It's saying the Moses was meeker than other men in the world.

Deuteronomy 6:15 *"(For the LORD thy God is a jealous God among you) lest the anger of the LORD thy God be kindled against thee, and destroy thee from off the face of the earth."*

Yahuah is reminding the Israelites that they were captives in Egypt, and if they continue serving pagan gods, He will remove them from their *land* and send them into captivity again. Sadly, that's what happened when the Assyrians, Babylonians, and Romans; were sent to desolate their land.

Deuteronomy 7:6 *"For thou art an holy people unto the LORD thy God: the LORD thy God hath chosen thee to be a special people unto himself, above all people that are upon the face of the earth."*

The Israelites were a set-apart people who were favored above gentiles in other *lands*.

1 Samuel 20:15 *"But also thou shalt not cut off thy kindness from my house forever: no, not when the LORD hath cut off the enemies of David every one from the face of the earth."*

David's enemies were cast down as they tried to control his *land*.

1 Kings 13:34 *"And this thing became sin unto the house of Jeroboam, even to cut it off, and to destroy it from off the face of the earth."*

1 Kings 13 lists the sins of Jeroboam, which deserved judgment. 1 Kings 14 declares that his son became sick and died. Thus Jeroboam's house, his lineage of a male successor, his control of the promised *land*, was ended.

Psalms 104:30 *"Thou sendest forth thy spirit, they are created: and thou renewest the face of the earth."*

Psalms 104:29 points to men dying, *"Thou hidest thy face, they are troubled: thou takest away their breath, they die, and return to their dust."* Psalms 104:30 seems to be proclaiming that though people die, that new generations are born who populate the *land*.

Jeremiah 25:26 *"And all the kings of the north, far and near, one with another, and all the kingdoms of the world, which are upon the face of the earth: and the king of Sheshach shall drink after them."*

It's saying that the kings rule the countries, the *lands*, of the world.

Jeremiah 28:16 *"Therefore thus saith the LORD; Behold, I will cast thee from off the face of the earth: this year thou shalt die, because thou hast taught rebellion against the LORD."*

Is He going to cast them off of the earth? No! They were removed from the *land*, from Jerusalem, when Nebuchadnezzar was sent to capture them.

Ezekiel 34:6 *"My sheep wandered through all the mountains, and upon every high hill: yea, my flock was scattered upon all the face of the earth, and none did search or seek after them."*

The previous verses say that they were scattered upon the *land* because there was no shepherd to guide them and protect them.

Ezekiel 38:20 *"So that the fishes of the sea, and the fowls of the heaven, and the beasts of the field, and all creeping things that creep upon the earth, and all the men that are upon the face of the earth, shall shake at my presence, and the mountains shall be thrown down, and the steep places shall fall, and every wall shall fall to the ground."*

The Strong's Hebrew word for *"earth"* is 127 *'adamah*; which means *soil (from its general redness): — country, earth, ground, land.* It's pointing to men who dwell on the *ground*, the *land*; not to the whole earth.

Ezekiel 39:14 *"And they shall sever out men of continual employment, passing through the land to bury with the passengers those that remain upon the face of the earth, to cleanse it: after the end of seven months shall they search."*

Ezekiel 39:11-13 is pointing to *Gog and his multitude* of people being buried, whose bodies are on the ground of the promised *land*.

Amos 9:6 *"It is he that buildeth his stories in the heaven, and hath founded his troop in the earth; he that calleth for the waters of the sea, and poureth them out upon the face of the earth: The LORD is his name."*

This is pointing back to the Genesis flooding of the earth, where water from the deep foundations was released to cover all of the *land* of the earth. We'll cover this verse in-depth in a future chapter.

Amos 9:8 *"Behold, the eyes of the Lord GOD are upon the sinful kingdom, and I will destroy it from off the face of the earth; saving that I will not utterly destroy the house of Jacob, saith the LORD."*

Was the nation of Israel removed off of the flat earth? No, it's saying that the Israelites would be desolated, but the remnant would be preserved. The next verse tells you that the house of Israel is spread out among the nations. *"For, lo, I will command, and I will sift the house of Israel among all nations, like as corn is sifted in a sieve, yet shall not the least grain fall upon the earth."* Amos 9:9

Zechariah 5:3 *"Then said he unto me, This is the curse that goeth forth over the face of the whole earth: for every one that stealeth shall be cut off as on this side according to it; and every one that sweareth shall be cut off as on that side according to it."*

The curse is against the *land* of Judea, for their breach of the law, contempt of the Gospel, and their rejection of the promised Messiah. The *land* was desolated by the Roman army in 70 AD.

Luke 12:56 *"Ye hypocrites, ye can discern the face of the sky and of the earth; but how is it that ye do not discern this time?"*

It's saying that they know how to look at the sky and clouds, to determine how the weather will be in the *land* of Judea. But they failed to understand the prophecies in Daniel 9:24-27, which foretold that their promised Messiah would appear at that time.

Luke 21:35 *"For as a snare shall it come on all them that dwell on the face of the whole earth."*

It can be argued that what Messiah described in Luke 21 took place in that generation, just as He proclaimed, *"Verily I say unto you, This generation shall not pass away, till all be fulfilled."* Luke 21:32

If so, then it's pointing to the *land* of Judea and the judgment of the Jews. If not, then a snare coming upon all people on the earth doesn't prove that it's flat.

These twenty-nine verses do not prove that the earth is flat or a globe. The word *face* (*paniym*) is simply pointing to the *ground*, the *land*, or a *country*; and the context of the verses shows that they're pointing to a particular area of *land*.

Nathan pushes his belief that the earth is flat onto Scripture, proclaiming that the word *face* points to a *geometrical flat surface*; but the verses did not validate his claim.

I can't comprehend this kind of logic, nor can I fathom flat-earthers sharing a list with these types of explanations; when the context of the verses tells another story.

"For the eyes of the Lord are over the righteous, and his ears are open unto their prayers: but the face of the Lord is against them that do evil."
1 Peter 3:12

CHAPTER 22

Waters have a Face (a geometrical flat surface)

Nathan cites Genesis 1:2, Genesis 7:18, Job 38:30

Nathan says in reference to Genesis 1:2, have you ever heard of the abyssal plains? Abyssal plains cover more than 50% of earth. Also they are some of the flattest smoothest areas on earth. It is impossible for the abyssal plains to cover more than 50% of the earth and for the earth to be a sphere, perhaps, the earth is "flat?"

Nathan is pushing his belief that *water is always flat* onto Scripture. The vast ocean abyssal plains, which are located in between the continents, don't have elevation changes. That doesn't prove that the earth is flat.

Genesis 1:2 *"And the earth was without form, and void; and darkness was upon the face of the deep. And the Spirit of God moved upon the face of the waters."*

The word *"face"* is pointing to the *"surface"* of the water, so it doesn't prove that the Earth is flat. The earth was covered in water, with no landmasses above the water.

Genesis 7:18 *"And the waters prevailed, and were increased greatly upon the earth; and the ark went upon the face of the waters."*

The ark was lifted off of the land onto the *surface* of the waters.

Job 38:30 *"The waters are hid as with a stone, and the face of the deep is frozen."*

It's saying that the *surface* of the water is frozen with ice so that it's as hard as a stone, which hides the waters below. These verses don't prove that the water has a flat geometric face. Flat-earthers, how do you defend these verses being on the list?

CHAPTER 23

Sky has a Face (a geometrical flat surface)

Nathan cites Matthew 16:3, Luke 12:56

No Scripture says that the sky has a geometric flat surface, that's just Nathan's eisegesis. The irony is that the sky on the flat earth model is curved under the dome, so it's not flat.

Matthew 16:3 *"And in the morning, it will be foul weather today: for the sky is red and lowering. O ye hypocrites, ye can discern the face of the sky; but can ye not discern the signs of the times?"*

Luke 12:56 *"Ye hypocrites, ye can discern the face of the sky and of the earth; but how is it that ye do not discern this time?"*

The word *"face"* is Strong's Greek 4383 *prosopon*, which means: *the front (as being towards view), i.e., the countenance, aspect, appearance, surface; by implication, presence, person:—(outward) appearance, before, countenance, face, fashion, (men's) person, presence.*

Matthew 16:3 says that the sky is *lowering*, pointing to the clouds, not the entire sky; so Nathan's point, that *the face of the sky is flat*, is invalid.

The context is about the Jewish leaders not understanding the fulfillment of the 70 weeks of Daniel 9 prophecy, which foretold exactly when their promised Messiah would appear. The disciples understood the prophecy and knew to look for Him.

"He (Andrew) first findeth his own brother Simon, and saith unto him, we have found the Messiah, which is, being interpreted, the Christ." John 1:41

"Philip findeth Nathanael, and saith unto him, we have found him, of whom Moses in the law, and the prophets, did write, Jesus of Nazareth, the son of Joseph." John 1:45

Matthew 16:3 and Luke 12:56 don't prove that the sky has a flat geometric face. Flat-earthers, how do you defend these verses being on the list?

"Through faith also Sara herself received strength to conceive seed, and was delivered of a child when she was past age, because she judged him faithful who had promised. Therefore sprang there even of one, and him as good as dead, so many as the stars of the sky in multitude, and as the sand which is by the sea shore innumerable."
Hebrews 11:11-12

CHAPTER 24

Earth has Ends

Nathan cites Deuteronomy 28:49, Deuteronomy 28:64, Deuteronomy 33:17, 1 Samuel 2:10, Job 37:3, Job 38:13, Psalm 46:9, Psalm 48:10, Psalm 59:13, Psalm 61:2, Psalm 65:5, Psalm 67:7, Psalm 72:8, Psalm 98:3, Psalm 135:7, Proverbs 8:29, Proverbs 17:24, Proverbs 30:4, Isaiah 5:26, Isaiah 26:15, Isaiah 40:28, Isaiah 41:5, Isaiah 41:9, Isaiah 42:10, Isaiah 43:6, Isaiah 45:22, Isaiah 48:20, Isaiah 49:6, Isaiah 52:10, Jeremiah 10:13, Jeremiah 16:19, Jeremiah 25:31, Jeremiah 25:33, Jeremiah 51:16, Daniel 4:22, Micah 5:4, Zechariah 9:10, Matthew 12:42, Luke 11:31, Acts 13:47

Flat-earthers say that a circular flat earth has ends, at the supposed ice wall; whereas a globe earth doesn't. They don't have any photographic proof of the ends of the flat earth, but they cite these verses anyway.

The word that is most often translated as *"earth"* in the Old Testament is Strong's Hebrew 776 *'erets* which means; *the earth: country, earth, field, ground, land, nations, way, wilderness, world.*

Genesis 1:10 gives us the definition, as it refers to the dry land as earth, *"And God called the dry land Earth; and the gathering together of the waters called he Seas: and God saw that it was good."*

The Hebrew word *erets* is used in these verses: Genesis 1:11-12 points to the *land* bringing forth grass and herbs; Genesis 1:24 refers to *land* beasts; Genesis 1:29 points to the herbs and trees growing on the *land*; Genesis 2:11 refers to the whole *land* of Havilah; and Genesis 30:25 points to a *country*.

The word *"end"* is Strong's Hebrew 7098 *qatsa; feminine of 7097,* which means *a termination; coast, corner, edge, lowest, uttermost.*

Strong's Hebrew *7097 qatseh;* means *an extremity: —after, border, brim, brink, edge, end, (in-)finite, frontier, outmost coast, quarter, shore, outside, some, ut(-ter-)most (part).*

The word *"ends"* points to an *extremity of land*. We see that with the end of our property, city, county, state, and country.

Keeping in mind that Nathan's premise in listing these verses is that only a flat earth has ends at the ice wall, let's look at them to see if they're pointing to the *end* of a flat earth ice wall, or simply to the *end* of an area of land.

Deuteronomy 28:49 *"The LORD shall bring a nation against thee from far, from the end of the earth, as swift as the eagle flieth; a nation whose tongue thou shalt not understand;"*

This verse points to the Babylonians and Romans who came from afar, to desolate Jerusalem. Did they come from an ice wall? No!

Deuteronomy 28:64 *"And the LORD shall scatter thee among all people, from the one end of the earth even unto the other; and there thou shalt serve other gods, which neither thou nor thy fathers have known, even wood and stone."*

It's pointing to the Father scattering the Israelites from one end of the earth even until the other. Did He put some on one side of an ice wall, and others on the opposite side of an ice wall? No!

Deuteronomy 33:17 *"with them he shall push the people together to the ends of the earth:"*

Is Yahuah pushing people to the ice wall of the flat earth? No, it's describing the Father causing the Israelites to push the Canaanites to the end of the *land* of Canaan.

1 Samuel 2:10 *"The adversaries of the LORD shall be broken to pieces; out of heaven shall he thunder upon them: the LORD shall judge the ends of the earth."*

Are we to believe that the Father is judging the flat earth ice wall? No!

Job 37:3 *"He directeth it under the whole heaven, and his lightning unto the ends of the earth."*

Is Yahuah casting lightning onto the flat earth ice wall? No!

Job 38:13 *"That it might take hold of the ends of the earth, that the wicked might be shaken out of it?"*

Are we to believe that the wicked people were shaken out of the ends of the flat earth, out of the ice wall? No!

Psalms 46:9 *"He maketh wars to cease unto the end of the earth; he breaketh the bow, and cutteth the spear in sunder; he burneth the chariot in the fire."*

It's pointing to a time of peace on the earth, with no wars going on.

Psalms 48:10 *"According to thy name, O God, so is thy praise unto the ends of the earth: thy right hand is full of righteousness."*

Yahuah should be praised all over the earth, but this isn't a flat earth proof.

Psalms 59:13 *"Consume them in wrath, consume them, that they may not be: and let them know that God ruleth in Jacob unto the ends of the earth. Selah."*

It's simply saying that Yahuah rules over all the earth.

Psalms 61:2 *"From the end of the earth will I cry unto thee, when my heart is overwhelmed: lead me to the rock that is higher than I."*

Is David crying from the end of the flat earth, from an ice wall? No!

Psalms 65:5 *"By terrible things in righteousness wilt thou answer us, O God of our salvation; who art the confidence of all the ends of the earth, and of them that are afar off upon the sea:"*

Is Yahuah the confidence of the ice wall of the flat earth? No! Yahuah is our salvation and our hope, but this is not a flat earth proof.

Psalms 67:7 *"God shall bless us; and all the ends of the earth shall fear him."*

Is it saying that the ends of the flat earth, the ice wall, fears Yahuah? No, it's saying that all of the peoples of the earth shall fear Him. Every knee will bow, and every tongue will confess Him.

Psalms 72:8 *"He shall have dominion also from sea to sea, and from the river unto the ends of the earth."*

It's simply saying that Yahuah's dominion is over all of the earth. Psalms 72:11 reinforces that His dominion is over all of the earth. *"Yea, all kings shall fall down before him: all nations shall serve him."* As does Psalms 72:19, *"And blessed be his glorious name for ever: and let the whole earth be filled with his glory; Amen, and Amen."*

Psalms 98:3 *"He hath remembered his mercy and his truth toward the house of Israel: all the ends of the earth have seen the salvation of our God."*

Is it saying that a flat earth ice wall has seen the salvation of Yahuah? No!

Psalms 135:7 *"He causeth the vapors to ascend from the ends of the earth; he maketh lightnings for the rain; he bringeth the wind out of his treasuries."*

Is it saying that vapors are ascending from the supposed ice wall? No, they ascend from the vast seas and oceans throughout the earth.

Proverbs 8:29 *"When he gave to the sea his decree, that the waters should not pass his commandment: when he appointed the foundations of the earth."*

Nathan seems to be pointing to the supposed flat earth ice wall, which doesn't allow waters to pass it; but it's simply saying that the water is bound, preventing it from overtaking the landmasses. Jeremiah 5:22 reinforces this point, *"Fear ye not me? saith the LORD: will ye not tremble at my presence, which have placed the sand for the bound of the sea by a perpetual decree, that it cannot pass it: and though the waves thereof toss themselves, yet can they not prevail; though they roar, yet can they not pass over it?"*

Proverbs 17:24 *"Wisdom is before him that hath understanding; but the eyes of a fool are in the ends of the earth."*

Are the eyes of a fool in the ends of the flat earth, at an ice wall? No!

Proverbs 30:4 *"Who hath ascended up into heaven, or descended? who hath gathered the wind in his fists? who hath bound the waters in a garment? who hath established all the ends of the earth? what is his name, and what is his son's name, if thou canst tell?"*

It's proclaiming that the waters are *bound*, hemmed in, by the land. Yahuah established the extremity (ends) of the earth (*eret*, land); so *"ends of the earth"* is referring to the shoreline, where dry land meets the sea.

Isaiah 5:26 *"And he will lift up an ensign to the nations from far, and will hiss unto them from the end of the earth: and, behold, they shall come with speed swiftly."*

Is Yahuah going to hiss unto the nations from the end of the flat earth, from an ice wall? No, He's saying that He's going to send the Babylonians against His people, for disobeying Him.

Isaiah 26:15 *"Thou hast increased the nation, O LORD, thou hast increased the nation: thou art glorified: thou hadst removed it far unto all the ends of the earth."*

Is Yahuah going to send His people to the end of the flat earth, the ice wall? No, it's saying that the Israelites were dispersed around the earth, and His set-apart saints have filled the nations.

Isaiah 40:28 *"Hast thou not known? Hast thou not heard that the everlasting God, the LORD, the Creator of the ends of the earth, fainteth not, neither is weary? there is no searching of his understanding."*

The fact that our Creator made the whole earth is not proof that it's flat. This is just Nathan pressing his flat earth beliefs onto the Scripture.

Isaiah 41:5 *"The isles saw it, and feared; the ends of the earth were afraid, drew near, and came."*

Did the ends of the flat earth, an ice wall, become *afraid* and *draw near*? No!

Isaiah 41:9 *"Thou whom I have taken from the ends of the earth, and called thee from the chief men thereof, and said unto thee, Thou art my servant; I have chosen thee, and not cast thee away."*

Is Yahuah going to take the Israelites from an ice wall? No!

Isaiah 42:10 *"Sing unto the LORD a new song, and his praise from the end of the earth, ye that go down to the sea, and all that is therein; the isles, and the inhabitants thereof."*

Are we to sing Yahuah's praises from the ice wall of the flat earth? No!

Isaiah 43:6 *"I will say to the north, Give up; and to the south, Keep not back: bring my sons from far, and my daughters from the ends of the earth."*

Is Yahuah going to bring daughters from a flat earth ice wall? No!

Isaiah 43:5-6 defines what the *"ends of the earth"* are, the four cardinal directions; north, east, south and west; *"Fear not: for I am with thee: I will bring thy seed from the east, and gather thee from the west. I will say to the north, Give up; and to the south, Keep not back: bring my sons from far, and my daughters from the ends of the earth"*

Isaiah 45:22 *"Look unto me, and be ye saved, all the ends of the earth: for I am God, and there is none else."*

Is Yahuah telling the ends of the flat earth, an ice wall, to look to Him and be saved? No!

Isaiah 48:20 *"Go ye forth of Babylon, flee ye from the Chaldeans, with a voice of singing declare ye, tell this, utter it even to the end of the earth; say ye, The LORD hath redeemed his servant Jacob."*

Is Yahuah telling the Jews to declare this unto the ice wall of the flat earth? No, it's describing a time of rejoicing when the Jews were released from captivity in the land of Babylon, to return home to Jerusalem.

Isaiah 49:6 *"And he said, It is a light thing that thou shouldest be my servant to raise up the tribes of Jacob, and to restore the preserved of Israel: I will also give thee for a light to the Gentiles, that thou mayest be my salvation unto the end of the earth."*

Amen, the Gospel should be preached all over the earth!

Isaiah 52:10 *"The LORD hath made bare his holy arm in the eyes of all the nations; and all the ends of the earth shall see the salvation of our God."*

Is an ice wall going to see the salvation of Yahuah? No!

Jeremiah 10:13 *"When he uttereth his voice, there is a multitude of waters in the heavens, and he causeth the vapors to ascend from the ends of the earth; he maketh lightnings with rain and bringeth forth the wind out of his treasures."*

Are the vapors ascending from an ice wall? No!

Jeremiah 16:19 *"O LORD, my strength, and my fortress, and my refuge in the day of affliction, the Gentiles shall come unto thee from the ends of the earth, and shall say, Surely our fathers have inherited lies, vanity, and things wherein there is no profit."*

Are the gentiles going to come from a flat earth ice wall? No!

Jeremiah 25:31 *"A noise shall come even to the ends of the earth; for the LORD hath a controversy with the nations, he will plead with all flesh; he will give them that are wicked to the sword, saith the LORD."*

Will Yahuah send the noise of a marching army from the end of the flat earth, the ice wall? No! The next verse points to wars in the nations, *"Thus saith the LORD of hosts, Behold, evil shall go forth from nation to nation, and a great whirlwind shall be raised up from the coasts of the earth."* Jeremiah 25:32

Jeremiah 25:33 *"And the slain of the LORD shall be at that day from one end of the earth even unto the other end of the earth: they shall not be lamented, neither gathered, nor buried; they shall be dung upon the ground."*

Were the slain laid out on the earth from one end of the flat earth ice wall to the other end of the flat earth ice wall? No!

It's talking about the bodies of slain Jews lying across the *land* of Judea, not the whole earth.

Jeremiah 51:16 *"When he uttereth his voice, there is a multitude of waters in the heavens; and he causeth the vapors to ascend from the ends of the earth: he maketh lightnings with rain, and bringeth forth the wind out of his treasures."*

Are the vapors ascending from an ice wall? No, they ascend from the vast oceans and seas of the earth.

Daniel 4:22 *"It is thou, O king, that art grown and become strong: for thy greatness is grown, and reacheth unto heaven, and thy dominion to the end of the earth."*

This is part of a dream which uses symbolism. It's pointing to the vast dominion of King Nebuchadnezzar, who ruled from Babylon; not to the end of a flat earth ice wall.

Micah 5:4 *"And he shall stand and feed in the strength of the LORD, in the majesty of the name of the LORD his God; and they shall abide: for now shall he be great unto the ends of the earth."*

Messiah is great unto the ends of the earth, but this verse isn't talking about the geographic boundaries of the flat earth model.

Matthew 12:42 / Luke 11:31 *"The queen of the south shall rise up in the judgment with this generation, and shall condemn it: for she came from the uttermost parts of the earth to hear the wisdom of Solomon; and, behold, a greater than Solomon is here."*

The queen of the south didn't come from a flat earth ice wall. She was from Sheba, which was a city and province of Arabia Felix.

Acts 13:47 *"For so hath the Lord commanded us, saying, I have set thee to be a light of the Gentiles, that thou shouldest be for salvation unto the ends of the earth.*

It's using symbolic language, to proclaim that the Gospel should be preached all over the world.

Do you see how ridiculous it is to proclaim that the verses in this section declare that the earth is flat? They're not pointing to the edge of the supposed flat Earth, to an ice wall. They're not talking about the shape of the earth at all.

I can't comprehend the mentality of Nathan, who has taken them out of their proper context, to declare that they point to a flat earth. Flat-earthers, how do you defend these verses being on the list?

"Now unto him that is able to do exceeding abundantly above all that we ask or think, according to the power that worketh in us, Unto him be glory in the church by Christ Jesus throughout all ages, world without end."
Ephesians 3:20-21

CHAPTER 25
Earth has 4 Corners/Quarters

Nathan cites Jeremiah 9:26, Jeremiah 25:23, Isaiah 11:12, Ezekiel 7:2, Ecclesiastes 1:6, Revelation 7:1, Revelation 20:8

Nathan asks, *"have you ever seen a spherically shaped sports ball, like a basketball or soccer ball, with a corner?"*

Geocentricworks.com proclaims, *"You cannot have corners on a sphere and that's because earth is not a sphere. Earth is Flat."*

They point out that a globe doesn't have corners, but how does a flat circle earth have corners? Some flat-earthers add corners to the outside edges, which are outside of the dome. That makes no sense as it negates their point about the supposed circle flat earth of Isaiah 40:22. You can't have it both ways!

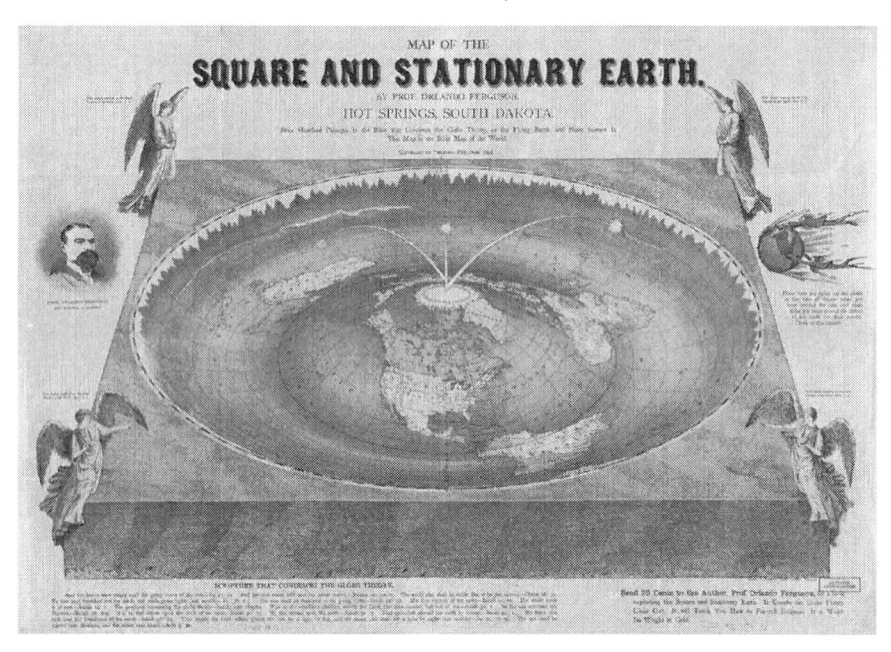

In the previous chapter, we saw that Isaiah 43:5-6 defined what the *"ends of the earth"* are, the four cardinal directions. *"Fear not: for I am with thee: I will bring thy seed from the east, and gather thee from the west. I will say to the north, Give up; and to the south, Keep not back: bring my sons from far, and my daughters from the ends of the earth."*

Genesis 13:14-15,17 describes the four directions, *"And the LORD said unto Abram, after that Lot was separated from him, Lift up now thine eyes, and look from the place where thou art northward, and southward, and eastward, and westward: For all the land which thou seest, to thee will I give it, and to thy seed for ever. Arise, walk through the land in the length of it and in the breadth of it; for I will give it unto thee."*

The same concept applies here to the four corners of the earth. The four universal coordinates of geography are north, east, south, and west; which are used in surveying and navigation. The four geographical directions form four quadrants; northeast, southeast, southwest, and northwest.

Let's look at the verses that Nathan cites about the *four corners* of the earth, to see if any prove that the earth is flat. I'm starting with Isaiah 11:12, because Nathan offers a different view of what the *"four corners"* are, which we can also apply to the other verses.

Isaiah 11:12 *"And he shall set up an ensign for the nations, and shall assemble the outcasts of Israel, and gather together the dispersed of Judah from the four corners of the earth."*

Were the outcasts of Israel and the dispersed of Judah living outside the dome, on the corners of the flat earth? No! Psalms 107:2-3 tells us that the redeemed saints are gathered from the four corners of the earth; north, east, south, and west. *"Let the redeemed of the LORD say so, whom he hath redeemed from the hand of the enemy; And gathered them out of the lands, from the east, and from the west, from the north, and from the south."*

In Nathan Roberts' *"Flat Earth Where are the 4 corners of the earth on the Gleason map?"* video, he cites Isaiah 11:12 as an example of a verse that points to four corners, and he said that *"when looking at this word "corners" you can come up with the word quarter."*

The problem is that the only Bible version that uses the word *"quarters"* for Isaiah 11:12 is the NIV, and it's not a good word-for-word translation. This is why Nathan picks and chooses which Bible version to use, as he selects the one which seems to imply what he wants to proclaim.

The Strong's Hebrew word for *"corner"* is 3671 *kanaph; an edge or extremity; specifically a wing, a flap, a quarter, a pinnacle, border, corner, end, feather, flying, overspreading, quarters, skirt, sort, uttermost part.*

Nathan created an explanation where the flat circle earth has four quarters, like a pie chart, which creates four corners.

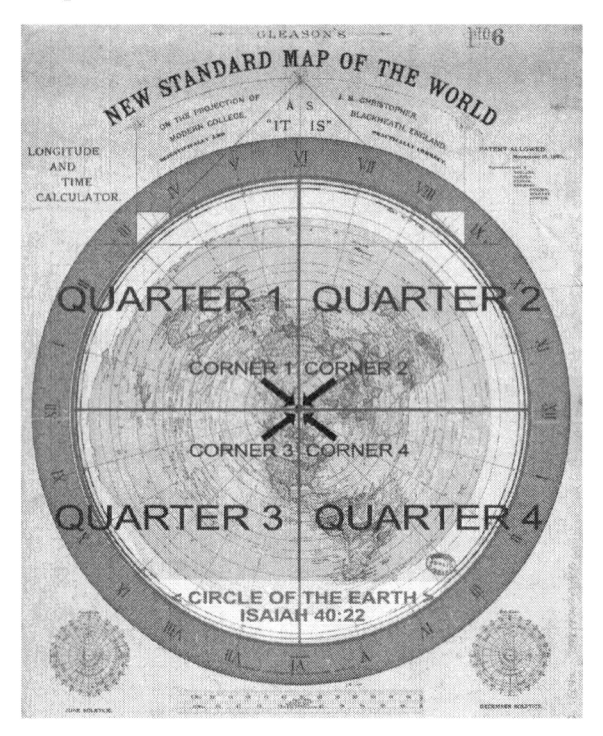

Nathan is effectively saying that the *"four corners of the earth"* meet at the North Pole. Are we to believe that the remnant of Israel is to be gathered from the area of the North Pole? No, so we can see that this explanation of the four corners is ridiculous!

The irony of Nathan using the *Gleason's New Standard Map Of The World* is that it's a north polar azimuthal equidistant projection of the globe earth. It's filed under US Patent No. 497,917; which reads *"The extorsion of the map from that of a globe consists, mainly in the straightening out of the meridian lines allowing each to retain their original value from Greenwich, the equator to the two poles."* From the patent description, we see that Gleason was in full knowledge that the map he created was simply a projection of the spherical earth.

1 Chronicles 9:24 tells us that the four quarters are the four directions. *"In four quarters were the porters, toward the east, west, north, and south."*

Isaiah 11:11 tells us where the remnant of Yahuah's people had been scattered, *"And it shall come to pass in that day, that the Lord shall set his hand again the second time to recover the remnant of his people, which shall be left, from Assyria, and from Egypt, and from Pathros, and from Cush, and from Elam, and from Shinar, and from Hamath, and from the islands of the sea."*

Though Nathan's explanation creates four corners on the flat earth map, it's an invalid theory. The obvious explanation is that the remnant of Yahuah was dispersed throughout the region; so they were north, east, south, and west; the four cardinal directions, the four corners of the earth.

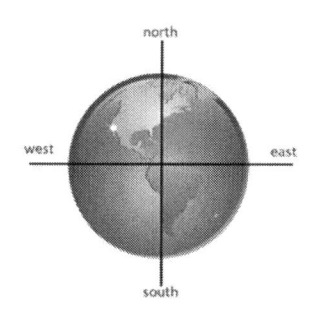

Daniel Valles in his Circle of the Earth Investigation, says, *"This is not referring to the cardinal points on a compass (North, etc.) because East and West have no end (Psalms 103:12)."*

The passages that are cited are not pointing to the whole earth, but an area of land. Does the land of Israel have an east end and a west end? Yes! Can people not be gathered from places that are east and west of a central location? Yes!

Jeremiah 9:26 *"Egypt, and Judah, and Edom, and the children of Ammon, and Moab, and all that are in the utmost corners, that dwell in the wilderness: for all these nations are uncircumcised, and all the house of Israel are uncircumcised in the heart."*

Are we to believe that Yahuah is going to punish people who live in the corners of the flat earth, outside the glass dome, or at the North Pole? No!

Jeremiah 25:23 *"Dedan, and Tema, and Buz, and all that are in the utmost corners,"*

This verse is simply saying that these people were from distant places, such as Edom, Arabia, and Mesopotamia.

The Hebrew word of *"corners"* in Jeremiah 9:26 and 25:23 is 6285 *pe'ah;* which means *properly, mouth in a figurative sense, i.e., direction, region, extremity:—corner, end, quarter, side.*

Here are a few verses which use the Hebrew word *pe'ah*, and they show that it's describing a direction; which reinforces that the four corners are the four cardinal directions. It's used for the north *side*, south *side*, west *side*, and east *side*, the four cardinal directions.

"And ye shall measure from without the city on the east side two thousand cubits, and on the south side two thousand cubits, and on the west side two thousand cubits, and on the north side two thousand cubits; and the city shall be in the midst: this shall be to them the suburbs of the cities." Numbers 35:5

"And these shall be the measures thereof; the north side four thousand and five hundred, and the south side four thousand and five hundred, and on the east side four thousand and five hundred, and the west side four thousand and five hundred." Ezekiel 48:16

Ezekiel 7:2 *"Also, thou son of man, thus saith the Lord GOD unto the land of Israel; An end, the end is come upon the four corners of the land."*

It's pointing to the *land* of Judea and the destruction of it, as Yahuah's judgment against the Israelites.

Ecclesiastes 1:6 *"The wind goeth toward the south, and turneth about unto the north; it whirleth about continually, and the wind returneth again according to his circuits."*

This verse doesn't say *"four corners,"* so I'm not sure why Nathan included it. Ecclesiastes 1:5 points to the sun rising in the east and setting in the west, *"The sun also ariseth, and the sun goeth down, and hasteth to his place where he arose."* Ecclesiastes 1:6 points to the directions of south and north; so once again we see that the *"four corners"* of the earth are the four cardinal directions.

Revelation 7:1 *"And after these things I saw four angels standing on the four corners of the earth, holding the four winds of the earth, that the wind should not blow on the earth, nor on the sea, nor on any tree."*

Are we to believe that the angels are holding back the four winds from the four corners of the flat earth, which is outside of the glass dome? No! Are we to believe that the angels are holding back the four winds from the four corners of the North Pole? No! It's simply saying that the angels are holding back judgment from the earth.

Revelation 20:8 *"And shall go out to deceive the nations which are in the four quarters of the earth, Gog and Magog, to gather them together to battle: the number of whom is as the sand of the sea."*

Are we supposed to believe that the armies of Gog and Magog are coming from the four corners of the flat earth, which is outside of the dome, or from the North Pole? No!

Genesis 28:14 tells us that Abraham's descendants were scattered all over the earth, naming the four directions, the four corners. *"And thy seed shall be as the dust of the earth, and thou shalt spread abroad to the west, and to the east, and to the north, and to the south: and in thee and in thy seed shall all the families of the earth be blessed."*

The following verses point to the four winds, the four cardinal directions.

"And upon Elam will I bring the four winds from the four quarters of heaven, and will scatter them toward all those winds; and there shall be no nation whither the outcasts of Elam shall not come." Jeremiah 49:36

"Then said he unto me, Prophesy unto the wind, prophesy, son of man, and say to the wind, Thus saith the Lord GOD; Come from the four winds, O breath, and breathe upon these slain, that they may live." Ezekiel 37:9

"Daniel spake and said, I saw in my vision by night, and, behold, the four winds of the heaven strove upon the great sea." Daniel 7:2

"Therefore the he goat waxed very great: and when he was strong, the great horn was broken; and for it came up four notable ones toward the four winds of heaven." Daniel 8:8

"And when he shall stand up, his kingdom shall be broken, and shall be divided toward the four winds of heaven; and not to his posterity, nor according to his dominion which he ruled: for his kingdom shall be plucked up, even for others beside those." Daniel 11:4

"Ho, ho, come forth, and flee from the land of the north, saith the Lord: for I have spread you abroad as the four winds of the heaven, saith the Lord." Zechariah 2:6

The Strong's Greek word for *"winds"* is 417 *anemos*; which means: *wind; (plural) by implication, (the four) quarters (of the earth).*

"And he shall send his angels with a great sound of a trumpet, and they shall gather together his elect from the four winds, from one end of heaven to the other." Matthew 24:31

"And then shall he send his angels, and shall gather together his elect from the four winds, from the uttermost part of the earth to the uttermost part of heaven." Mark 13:27

Luke 13:29 points to a time when the set-apart saints are gathered from the four corners of the earth. *"And they shall come from the east, and from the west, and from the north, and from the south, and shall sit down in the kingdom of God."*

Scripture declares that the four corners are the four cardinal directions: north, east, south, and west. None of these verses prove that the earth is flat. Flat-earthers, how do you defend these verses being on the list?

CHAPTER 26

The Firmament/Dome/Vaulted Dome, and expanse created thereby and upon where God's throne exists.

Nathan cites Genesis 1:6-8, Genesis 1:14-18, Genesis 1:20, Genesis 7:11, Genesis 8:2, Job 9:8, Job 26:7, Job 28:24, Job 37:3, Job 37:18, Psalm 19:1, Psalm 150:1, Proverbs 8:28, Isaiah 40:22, Isaiah 42:5, Isaiah 44:24, Isaiah 45:12, Isaiah 48:13, Ezekiel 1:22-26, Ezekiel 10:1, Daniel 12:3, Amos 9:6, Acts 7:56, Revelation 4:6, Revelation 6:14

Nathan adds: With understanding the properties of water, it requires a physically hardened substance to keep it contained. Thus, a dome/firmament is not only logic but is within the proper context of scripture.

Do clouds have a *'hard substance'* to be able to hold water? No! We see that a *"physically hardened substance"* is not required to hold water, which invalidates Nathan's logic in pointing to a glass dome.

2 Samuel 22:12 says, *"And he made darkness pavilions round about him, dark waters, and thick clouds of the skies."* Job 26:8 says, *"He bindeth up the waters in his thick clouds; and the cloud is not rent under them."* Job 38:34 says, *"Canst thou lift up thy voice to the clouds, that abundance of waters may cover thee?"* Ecclesiastes 11:3 says, *"If the clouds be full of rain, they empty themselves upon the earth: and if the tree fall toward the south, or toward the north, in the place where the tree falleth, there it shall be."*

Nathan proclaims that Yahuah's throne sits on top of the glass dome, but Scripture never says that. 1 Kings 22:19, 2 Chronicles 18:18, Psalms 11:4, Psalms 103:19 and Isaiah 6:1, talk about Yahuah's throne, and none of them proclaim that it sits on a dome.

Thirty verses in Revelation mention Yahuah's throne, and not one of them declares that it sits on a glass dome. Nathan's assertion is without merit, so let's see what the verses that he listed are saying.

Genesis 1:6-8 *"And God said, Let there be a firmament in the midst of the waters, and let it divide the waters from the waters. And God made the firmament, and divided the waters which were under the firmament from the waters which were above the firmament: and it was so. And God called the firmament Heaven. And the evening and the morning were the second day."*

Genesis 1:8 gives us the definition of the word *"firmament"* = *"heaven."* Is a glass dome called heaven? No! Is the *expanse* above the earth, the *sky*, called *heaven*? Yes! Genesis 1:8 in the Interlinear Bible reads, *"And so God called the sky the firmament. And there was evening and morning, the second day."*

Psalms 148:4 tells us that the waters are above the heavens, confirming that the *firmament* is the expanse of the heavens, *"Praise him, ye heavens of heavens, and ye waters that be above the heavens."*

In his introduction, Nathan said that he was going to cite Websters 1828 Dictionary, Easton's Bible Dictionary, Naves Topical Index and the Smith's Bible Dictionary; so why didn't he include those definitions here? It's because they don't reinforce his belief in a glass dome firmament, and they declare that *the firmament is the expanse of the heavens.*

Webster's 1828 Dictionary defines *firmament*: *The region of the air; the sky or heavens. In scripture, the word denotes an expanse, a wide extent; for such is the signification of the Hebrew word, coinciding with regio, region, and reach. The original therefore does not convey the sense of solidity, but of stretching, extension; the great arch or expanse over our heads, in which are placed the atmosphere and the clouds, and in which the stars appear to be placed, and are seen.*

Easton's Bible Dictionary defines *firmament*: *This word means simply "expansion." It denotes the space or expanse like an arch appearing immediately above us.*

Naves Topical Index defines *firmament*: *The expanse above the earth.*

Smith's Bible Dictionary defines *firmament*: *The word denotes an expanse, a wide extent. The original, therefore, does not convey the sense of solidity, but of stretching, extension; the great arch of expanse over our heads, in which are placed the atmosphere and the clouds, and in which the stars appear to be placed, and are really seen.*

In his book, in talking about the firmament, Nathan tells us to go outside and look at the firmament which is over our head. The irony is that you see the *expanse* of the *heavens*, the *sky*, but you don't see a glass dome. And flat-earthers don't have any pictures of the glass dome.

Nathan says that many English Bible translations use the word *"dome"* not *"firmament,"* but then he fails to list them. I found two out of more than two dozen translations; the Contemporary English Version and the New Revised Standard Version. Two hardly counts as *"many."*

The KJ3 Literal Translation Bible uses the word *"expanse"* not *"firmament."* "And God said, Let an expanse be in the midst of the waters, and let it be dividing between the waters and waters. And God made the expanse, and He separated between the waters which were under the expanse and the waters which were above the expanses. And it was so. And God called the expanse, Heavens. And it was evening, and it was morning, a second day."

The Hebrew word for *heaven* is 8064 *shamayim*. It points to two levels of heaven, the visible arch in which the clouds move, as well as the higher ether where the celestial bodies are located.

Easton's Bible Dictionary defines *heaven* as: *The usual Hebrew word for "heavens" is shamayim, a plural form meaning "heights, "elevations."*

Smith's Bible Dictionary defines heaven as: *This (shamayim) is the word used in the expression "the heaven and the earth," or "the upper and lower regions."*

The Hebrew word for *firmament* is 7549 *raqiy* from 7554; which means *properly, an expanse, i.e., the firmament or (apparently) visible arch of the sky.*

The firmament is not a glass dome. Yahuah called the *firmament, heaven*. Scripture declares that the definition of *heaven* is the *sky*.

The heavenly sky is not just empty space; it has *ether*, it has substance; which is what Sir Isaac Newton, Nikola Tesla, and others, describe in the expanse around the globe earth.

Scripture defines three levels of heaven: the expanse in which the birds fly and the clouds hold vast amounts of water to nourish the earth; the airy and starry heavens; and the third heaven, the residence of Yahuah and angels.

The argument that the firmament is an enormous glass dome that covers the whole earth shouldn't even be proposed as an option.

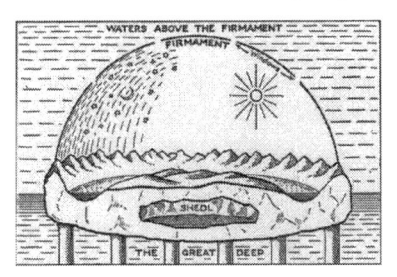

Scripturally, a glass dome has no merit. Flat-earthers have to force an explanation to justify the glass dome. They point to the Hebrew root word 7554 *raqa*, to proclaim that the firmament is a glass dome.

It's a primitive root word which means; *to pound the earth (as a sign of passion); by analogy to expand (by hammering); by implication, to overlay (with thin sheets of metal):—beat, make broad, spread abroad (forth, over, out, into plates), stamp, stretch.*

The idea is to beat metal into thin plates, to stretch the metal; for example, to cover the altar in Numbers 16:39. *"And Eleazar the priest took the brasen censers, wherewith they that were burnt had offered; and they were made broad plates for a covering of the altar:"*

The verses that are cited by Nathan clearly show that what's being stretched is not a glass dome, as that's not even made up of metal; but rather that the *heavens are stretched*.

If the writers of the Scriptures wanted to specifically proclaim that the *firmament* was like stretched metal, they would have used Hebrew 7554 *raqa* as the primary word, but they didn't. They used Hebrew 7549 *raqiy*, which is the *expanse of the heavens*.

Since flat-earthers rely so heavily on the Hebrew word <u>raqa</u>, let's look to see if it was used to describe stretched glass?

"<u>And they did beat the gold</u> into thin plates, and cut it into wires, to work it in the blue, and in the purple, and in the scarlet, and in the fine linen, with cunning work." Exodus 39:3

"And Eleazar the priest took the brasen censers, wherewith they that were burnt had offered; and <u>they were made broad plates</u> for a covering of the altar:" Numbers 16:39

"Then did I beat them as small as the dust of the earth, I did stamp them as the mire of the street, and <u>did spread them abroad</u>." 2 Samuel 22:43

"<u>To him that stretched out the earth</u> above the waters: for his mercy endureth for ever." Psalms 136:6

"The workman melteth a graven image, and the goldsmith <u>spreadeth it over with gold</u>, and casteth silver chains." Isaiah 40:19

"Silver <u>spread into plates</u> is brought from Tarshish, and gold from Uphaz, the work of the workman, and of the hands of the founder: blue and purple is their clothing: they are all the work of cunning men." Jeremiah 10:9

"Thus saith the Lord GOD; Smite with thine hand, and <u>stamp with thy foot</u>, and say, Alas for all the evil abominations of the house of Israel! for they shall fall by the sword, by the famine, and by the pestilence." Ezekiel 6:11

"For thus saith the Lord GOD; Because thou hast clapped thine hands, and <u>stamped with the feet</u>, and rejoiced in heart with all thy despite against the land of Israel;" Ezekiel 25:6

None of these verses point to stretching out glass. A few refer to pounding metal to stretch it out over items in the temple.

The *arch of the sky* doesn't point to a glass dome, it's speaking about our visual perspective as we look out at the sky from horizon to horizon, and it appears like an arch.

The heavens are arched, bowed; not a glass dome. *"He bowed the heavens also, and came down: and darkness was under his feet."* Psalms 18:9. *"Bow thy heavens, O LORD, and come down: touch the mountains, and they shall smoke."* Psalms 144:5

The whole narrative of the firmament being a stretched glass dome is built on a false foundation. All of these verses declare that it is the *"heavens"* which are *stretched out*, not a glass dome.

"Which alone <u>spreadeth out the heavens</u>, and treadeth upon the waves of the sea." Job 9:8

"Who coverest thyself with light as with a garment: who <u>stretchest out the heavens</u> like a curtain." Psalms 104:2

"Thus saith God the LORD, he that created the heavens, and stretched them out; he that spread forth the earth, and that which cometh out of it; he that giveth breath unto the people upon it, and spirit to them that walk therein." Isaiah 42:5

"Thus saith the LORD, thy redeemer, and he that formed thee from the womb, I am the LORD that maketh all things; that stretcheth forth the heavens alone; that spreadeth abroad the earth by myself;" Isaiah 44:24

"I have made the earth, and created man upon it: I, even my hands, have stretched out the heavens, and all their host have I commanded." Isaiah 45:12

"And forgettest the LORD thy maker, that hath stretched forth the heavens, and laid the foundations of the earth; and hast feared continually every day because of the fury of the oppressor, as if he were ready to destroy? and where is the fury of the oppressor?" Isaiah 51:13

"He hath made the earth by his power, he hath established the world by his wisdom, and hath stretched out the heavens by his discretion." Jeremiah 10:12

"He hath made the earth by his power, he hath established the world by his wisdom, and hath stretched out the heaven by his understanding." Jeremiah 51:15

"The burden of the word of the LORD for Israel, saith the LORD, which stretcheth forth the heavens, and layeth the foundation of the earth, and formeth the spirit of man within him." Zechariah 12:1

When the earth was formed, there was no atmosphere, no protection. The heavens were created and stretched out, to provide a protective atmosphere and an expansive area for the clouds and the birds of the air. The second level of the heavens contains the stars, sun, and moon.

Genesis 1:14-18 *"And God said, Let there be lights in the firmament of the heaven to divide the day from the night; and let them be for signs, and for seasons, and for days, and years: And let them be for lights in the firmament of the heaven to give light upon the earth: and it was so. And God made two great lights; the greater light to rule the day, and the lesser light to rule the night: he made the stars also. And God set them in the firmament of the heaven to give light upon the earth, and to rule over the day and over the night,* and to divide the light from the darkness: and God saw that it was good.*"*

The KJ3 Literal Translation Bible uses the word *"expanse"* not *"firmament."* Are the sun and moon not in the *expanse of heaven*? Yes! So this isn't a flat earth proof.

Nathan rationalizes that the earth was created first, then the sun; so that proves the flat earth. He's saying that if the heliocentric globe earth model is correct, then the sun would have been created first, and then the earth to orbit around it. That's a valid point, but a geocentric globe earth could have been created first, and then the sun and moon to orbit it; so it's not a flat-earth proof.

Genesis 1:20 *"And God said, Let the waters bring forth abundantly the moving creature that hath life, and fowl that may fly above the earth in the open firmament of heaven."*

Is a glass dome over a flat earth *"open"*? No, it's a closed ecosystem. Flat-earthers argue that there's open space *under* the dome, but the text is describing the *firmament*. A glass dome is an enclosure, so it's not open.

Genesis 1:8 gives us the definition of the word *"firmament"* = *"heaven." "And God called the firmament Heaven."* Genesis 1:20 is saying that birds fly in the *sky*, in the *open expanse of heaven*.

By this, we can see that the *"open firmament"* is the *open expanse* of the heavens.

Genesis 7:11 *"In the six hundredth year of Noah's life, in the second month, the seventeenth day of the month, the same day were all the fountains of the great deep broken up, and the windows of heaven were opened."*

Are we to believe that a glass dome has windows? No! The text isn't saying that the *windows of the firmament* were opened, but that the *windows of heaven* were opened up.

Before the flood, people lived much longer. The Bible says that Noah lived to 950 years, Methuselah lived 969 years, Jared 962 years, and Mahalaleel 895 years.

After the flood, Genesis 6:3 says that the human lifespan was reduced dramatically down to 120 years. *"Then the LORD said, "My Spirit shall not strive with man forever, because he also is flesh; nevertheless his days shall be one hundred and twenty years."*

So what changed? During the pre-flood era, the earth enjoyed a warm tropical environment, which had enhanced oxygen in the atmosphere. Organisms grew larger and lived longer as a result, and people lived longer too.

Many creationists have attributed this to a water vapor canopy that was formed by Yahuah on the second day, the *"waters above the firmament"* (Genesis 1:7). This theory holds that a vast blanket of water vapor, translucent to the light of the sun and stars, created a marvelous greenhouse effect which maintained mild temperatures from pole to pole.

Citing evidence of a denser atmosphere in the past, Henry M. Morris postulates that this vapor layer would have dramatically increased the atmospheric pressure on the surface of the early earth, again contributing to a healthier environment (like a natural hyperbaric chamber).

He says that it would certainly have had the further effect of efficiently filtering harmful radiation from space, markedly reducing the rate of somatic mutations in living cells, and, as a consequence, drastically decreasing the rate of aging and death. (1)

After the water canopy collapsed, as the *"windows of heaven"* were opened to help flood the earth, the canopy was either no longer in place or significantly reduced in size. Ever since then, the earth has been subjected to more of the sun's harmful rays and has reduced oxygen density, resulting in the dramatic drop-off in longevity.

Pastor Dean Odle cites Psalms 148:4 to proclaim that the waters above the firmament are still in place. *"Praise him, ye heavens of heavens, and ye waters that be above the heavens."* But his explanation misses the mark, as David is pointing to the waters above the heavens, not above a glass dome firmament.

There's vapors, rain, snow, and hail; stored up in the clouds of the expanse of heaven. They're mentioned four verses later in Psalms 148:8 *"Fire, and hail; snow, and vapour; stormy wind fulfilling his word."*

The water vapor canopy wouldn't have contained enough water to flood the whole earth, so the rest would have come from the *"fountains of the great deep."*

Genesis 1:2 says that deep water covered the earth so that no land was seen; much like when the earth was flooded in the days of Noah. *"And the earth was without form, and void; and darkness was upon the face of the deep. And the Spirit of God moved upon the face of the waters."*

Genesis 1:9-10 describes how much of the water was removed from the surface of the earth and gathered underground, which allowed dry land to appear.

"And God said, Let the waters under the heaven be gathered together unto one place, and let the dry land appear: and it was so. And God called the dry land Earth; and the gathering together of the waters called the Seas: and God saw that it was good. "

The Strong's Hebrew word for *"seas"* is *yam;* which means: *to roar; a sea or <u>large body of water</u>; specifically, the Mediterranean Sea; sometimes a large river, or an artificial basin; locally, the west, or the south:—sea, south, west.*

Genesis is pointing to a large body of water that is stored under the earth, the *"fountains of the deep,"* which were used to flood the earth, and then returned underground. *"The fountains also of the deep and the windows of heaven were stopped, and the rain from heaven was restrained; And the waters returned from off the earth continually: and after the end of the hundred and fifty days the waters were abated."* Genesis 8:2-3

We can see how the deep fountains were *'compassed'* under layers of the globe earth, which was then opened up to help flood the earth, coming to an end after 40 days and nights. And we can see how this event is directly linked to the reduced lifespan of people.

Flat-earthers argue that the water that flooded the earth during the days of Noah was above the glass dome, but that doesn't explain why people lived longer before the flood.

It wouldn't have protected people from the sun's harmful radiation because the sun is under the dome. And it wouldn't have changed the earth's environment.

The concept of a giant glass dome that spans over 196,900,000 square miles of the earth is ridiculous enough, but add the pressure of all that water on top of it, and it becomes absurd.

Genesis 8:2 *"The fountains also of the deep and the windows of heaven were stopped, and the rain from heaven was restrained."*

If Genesis 7:11 is pointing to literal windows on a glass dome being opened, then we would think that this verse would say that they were *"closed,"* but it uses the word *"stopped"* which means that the canopy of water ceased to pour water on the earth.

Job 9:8 *"Which alone spreadeth out the heavens, and treadeth upon the waves of the sea."*

The Hebrew word for *"spreadeth"* is 5186 *natah; to stretch or spread out; by implication, to bend away; used in a great variety of application (as follows): afternoon, apply, bow, carry aside, decline, deliver, extend, go down, be gone, incline, intend, lay, let down, offer, outstretched, overthrown, pervert, pitch, prolong, put away, shew, spread, stretch, take, turn, wrest, cause to yield.*

That is the same concept that we saw in Genesis 1:7, where the *"firmament,"* the heavens, were *spread out*. Flat-earthers point to metal being pounded to spread it out, to fabricate the explanation that glass was spread out over the earth. But Job 9:8 is telling us that it is the *heavens* which were *spread out*, not a glass dome. How are they ignoring the clear statements of Yahuah's Word? It's telling us that the *firmament* is the *expanse of heavens*, which was *spread out* over the earth.

Job 26:7 *"He stretcheth out the north over the empty place, and hangeth the earth upon nothing."*

Nathan adds: From the "north" is being "stretched" over what empty place?

Nathan proclaims that there are *pillars* under the earth to support it so that the earth doesn't need to hang from anything.

The verses that he cited aren't pointing to physical pillars; and it's absurd to say that a flat earth is on pillars, which sit on nothing.

We previously saw that the Hebrew word for *hangs* is 8518 *talah;* which means *to suspend, to hang (up)*. In twenty-six other verses where *talah* is used, they all refer to something that is suspended from above, such as people who have been hanged; and none of them point to the object being supported by something below.

A flat earth or a globe earth can be held in place by Yahuah, *hanging from nothing*, so this it doesn't prove that the earth is flat.

But let's explore it more because it's an interesting verse. What's being stretched? Looking back to the many verses which say that it's the *heavens which are stretched out*, it makes sense to apply that here too. Recall what Isaiah 40:22 says, *"It is he that sitteth upon the circle of the earth, and the inhabitants thereof are as grasshoppers; that stretcheth out the heavens as a curtain, and spreadeth them out as a tent to dwell in."*

We can see that the *"circle"* is the ecliptic circle that surrounds the globe earth. Twelve primary constellations are located on the ecliptic *circle*, and the globe earth is surrounded by a canopy of stars as thirty-six decan constellations fill the skies from the north celestial pole to the south celestial pole.

What Job is proclaiming is *"stretched out"* is the whole celestial sphere, which is like a *curtain*, or *canopy*, or *tent*, around the earth. This is the *tabernacle* in which Yahuah dwells.

Look at the cover of the book, and you see that the celestial sphere of stars rotates around the north celestial pole star. Below it is a vast *empty space* inside of the planisphere. In the middle of that canopy of stars is the globe earth, the jewel of the universe, which is *hung upon nothing*.

It's really interesting that Isaiah's narrative of Lucifer's fall also includes the word *"north."* *"How art thou fallen from heaven, O Lucifer, son of the morning! how art thou cut down to the ground, which didst weaken the nations! For thou hast said in thine heart, I will ascend into heaven, I will exalt my throne above the stars of God: I will sit also upon the mount of the congregation, in the sides of the north: I will ascend above the heights of the clouds; I will be like the most High."* Isaiah 14:12-14

The context of Isaiah 14 is about the Babylonian kingdom, which Satan used to create the narrative of pagan god worship; of the sun god Nimrod, the moon goddess Semiramis, and their supposed incarnate christ child Tammuz. From this came the Egyptian sun god Osiris, moon goddess Isis, and their supposed incarnate christ child Horus.

Satan used the Babylonian kingdom to deceive the nations into pagan god worship and into building a tower which would reach to the heavens. Satan desires to steal glory from the Heavenly Father, and to exalt his throne above the earth; to be like the most High and have his throne above the North Star where the Heavenly Father's throne resides.

Read the book *The Witness of the Stars* by E.W. Bullinger, and you see that the constellation of Cephus is at the top of the circle, near the north celestial pole star.

In the constellation of Cephus, we see the glorious, crowned, enthroned king (our Messiah) in the highest heaven. He has a scepter in his hand and his foot planted on the north celestial pole star. HalleluYah!

Hebrews 1:8 says, *"But unto the Son he saith, Thy throne, O God, is for ever and ever: a sceptre of righteousness is the sceptre of thy kingdom."*

Also near the north celestial pole star is the constellation of Draco, the dragon, Satan, the enemy of Messiah. We just read how Satan sought to take the throne of heaven. Are your eyes opening up?

There's a lot more represented in the stars than we've been taught. The enemy has perverted the narrative of the constellations to make them about pagan gods, astrology, and fortune-telling; but the astronomy of the stars was created by Yahuah in the beginning to foretell the battle between good and evil, and to proclaim the redemption of the set-apart saints.

Cephus means *the one cometh to rule, the branch, the king.* Jeremiah 23:5 says, *"Behold, the days are coming," declares the LORD, "When I will raise up for David a righteous Branch; And He will reign as king and act wisely And do justice and righteousness in the land."* Other verses that point to Messiah as the *"branch"* are Isaiah 4:2, Isaiah 11:1-5, Jeremiah 33:15-16, Zechariah 3:8, and Zechariah 6:12-13. HalleluYah!

Luke 19:38 points to Messiah as the King, *"Saying, blessed be the King that cometh in the name of the Lord: peace in heaven, and glory in the highest."*

Many other verses point to Messiah as King, but I can't leave out John 18:37, *"Pilate therefore said unto him, Art thou a king then? Jesus answered, Thou sayest that I am a king. To this end was I born, and for this cause came I into the world, that I should bear witness unto the truth. Every one that is of the truth heareth my voice."* HalleluYah!

The brightest star in the constellation of Cephus is called *Al Deramin*, which means *come quickly*. The next brightest is *Al Phirk*, which means *the Redeemer*. The next brightest is called *Al Rai*, which means *who bruises or breaks*. All of the stars describe our beloved Messiah and His role in our redemption. Psalms 147:4 says, *"He appoints the number of the stars, He gives names to all of them."*

Keeping the constellation of Cephus in mind, which represents Messiah sitting on a throne with His foot on the north celestial pole star, which is on top of the whole celestial sphere being as a footstool under His foot; read Hebrews 1:10-13. *"And, Thou, Lord, in the beginning hast laid the foundation of the earth; and the heavens are the works of thine hands: They shall perish; but thou remainest; and they all shall wax old as doth a garment; And as a vesture shalt thou fold them up, and they shall be changed: but thou art the same, and thy years shall not fail. But to which of the angels said he at any time, Sit on my right hand, until I make thine enemies thy footstool?"*

The demise of Lucifer is depicted in a key way with the astronomical mechanism known as *the precession of the poles*. Alpha Draconis (Thuban), the brightest star in Draco the dragon, was the original pole star. But due to the precession of the poles, the pole star has moved from Draco and now resides near Polaris or Al Ruccaba of Ursa Minor. (2)

Al Ruccaba means *the turned* or *ridden on*. The North Polar star is now under Messiah's feet, for His death and resurrection defeated the enemy. Ephesians 1:20-23 points to Messiah being given authority, as Satan had it on earth beforehand.

"Which he wrought in Christ, when he raised him from the dead, and set him at his own right hand in the heavenly places, Far above all principality, and power, and might, and dominion, and every name that is named, not only in this world, but also in that which is to come: And hath put all things under his feet, and gave him to be the head over all things to the church, Which is his body, the fulness of him that filleth all in all."

Messiah is represented in Cephus and Satan is represented in Draco, but what about Ursa Minor which has the North Polar Star at the end of its tail? Ursa Minor is called the *Little Bear,* or the *Lesser Bear*. That name is a deception to hide what it means, as it's pointing to the saints, the *Lesser Fold,* the *little flock of sheep.* These are those who have been *'partakers of the heavenly calling'* to overcome the enemy.

John 10:14-16 points to this lesser fold, *"I am the good shepherd, and know my sheep, and am known of mine. As the Father knoweth me, even so know I the Father: and I lay down my life for the sheep. And other sheep I have, which are not of this fold: them also I must bring, and they shall hear my voice; and there shall be one fold, and one shepherd."*

Who does Satan, Draco, war against? The saints, Messiah's fold of sheep. *"And there appeared another wonder in heaven; and behold a great red dragon (Draco), having seven heads and ten horns, and seven crowns upon his heads. And his tail drew the third part of the stars of heaven, and did cast them to the earth: and the dragon stood before the woman which was ready to be delivered, for to devour her child as soon as it was born. And she brought forth a man child, who was to rule all nations with a rod of iron: and her child was caught up unto God, and to his throne."* Revelation 12:3-5

"And the dragon was wroth with the woman, and went to make war with the remnant of her seed, which keep the commandments of God, and have the testimony of Jesus Christ." Revelation 12:17

Alpha in the constellation of Draco was the North Polar star when the zodiac was first formed, which represented Satan's authority on earth. But the pole star is now Alpha in the constellation that represents the *little fold*, Messiah's saints, who have the authority to overcome the dragon by the power of their Messiah. HalleluYah!

Revelation 12:11 proclaims the victory of the saints over the Dragon. *"And they overcame him by the blood of the Lamb, and by the word of their testimony; and they loved not their lives unto the death."*

The whole celestial sphere rotates around the north celestial pole star to tell the story of our redemption. Are you seeing how the enemy has hidden this story by creating pagan imagery? Are you seeing that the story is written in the whole celestial sphere, proving that the earth is a globe?

The thirty-six constellations wrap around the earth in a planisphere, a global sphere that surrounds the earth. Programs such as Stellarium and the SkyView phone app, let you see the whole celestial sphere in real-time. Flat-earthers may say that it's fake programming, but we can see in real life exactly what they show on the screen. There's no way to fake that.

Sadly, Pastors have been misled about astronomy, condemning it with a false association to astrology. People have understood the planisphere of stars for many thousands of years. Job clearly understood the stars and their meaning.

Christians wrote the following books when there wasn't any debate about the flat earth, so they had no agenda. They were simply proclaiming the glory of the sphere of stars which surrounds the globe earth, which tells the redemption story. **God's Voice in the Stars**: *Zodiac Signs and Bible Truth* by Ken Fleming; *The Witness Of The Stars* by E.W. Bullinger; and *The Gospel in the Stars* by Joseph A. Seiss.

All that said, Job 26:7 is a proof of the globe earth and the planisphere of constellations around it; the *firmament* of the *expanse* of *heaven*, the *curtain* of stars, the *tabernacle* of Yahuah.

Job 28:24 *"For he looketh to the ends of the earth, and seeth under the whole heaven;"*

How does this verse prove that there's a glass dome over a flat earth? It's proclaiming that Yahuah, who is all-powerful and all-seeing, views the earth and the whole celestial sphere of stars.

Job 37:3 *"He directeth it under the whole heaven, and his lightning unto the ends of the earth."*

How does this verse prove that there's a glass dome over a flat earth? The *"ends of the earth"* is not proof of a flat disc earth, but rather it's symbolizing that His voice is heard throughout the earth.

Job 37:18 *"Hast thou with him spread (raqa) out the sky, which is strong, and as a molten looking glass?"*

Nathan adds: The premise of this verse is a "question" being posed, in order to put "man" in perspective to the Creator. In that teaching moment, Yahuah reveals a truth about the "expanse," that it is "strong" just like a "molten looking glass."

Once again Scripture is declaring that *the sky is spread out*, not a dome. It says *"as a molten looking glass,"* so it's a simile that's not declaring that the sky is actually made of glass. Nathan is intermixing the words *"sky, heaven,* and *firmament;"* to imply that it's pointing to a glass dome, but that's intellectually dishonest.

The Hebrew word for *"sky"* is 7834 *shachaq;* which means *a powder (as beaten small): by analogy, a thin vapor; by extension, the firmament: — cloud, small dust, heaven, sky.* Read these verses which use the word *shachaq,* and see how many times they describe a glass dome.

"There is none like unto the God of Jeshurun, who rideth upon the heaven in thy help, and in his excellency *on the sky*." Deuteronomy 33:26

"And he made darkness pavilions round about him, dark waters, and thick clouds *of the skies*." 2 Samuel 22:12

"Look unto the heavens, and see; and behold *the clouds* which are higher than thou." Job 35:5

"*Which the clouds* do drop and distill upon man abundantly" Job 36:28

"And now men see not the bright light *which is in the clouds*: but the wind passeth, and cleanseth them." Job 37:21

"Who can number *the clouds* in wisdom? or who can stay the bottles of heaven," Job 38:37

"He made darkness his secret place; his pavilion round about him were dark waters and thick clouds *of the skies*." Psalms 18:11

"Thy mercy, O LORD, is in the heavens; and thy faithfulness *reacheth unto the clouds.*" Psalms 36:5

"For thy mercy is great unto the heavens, and thy truth *unto the clouds*." Psalms 57:10

"Ascribe ye strength unto God: his excellency is over Israel, and his strength *is in the clouds*." Psalms 68:34

"The clouds poured out water: *the skies* sent out a sound: thine arrows also went abroad." Psalms 77:17

"Though he had commanded *the clouds* from above, and opened the doors of heaven," Psalms 78:23

"*For who in the heaven* can be compared unto the LORD? who among the sons of the mighty can be likened unto the LORD?" Psalms 89:6

"It shall be established for ever as the moon, and as a faithful witness in heaven. *Selah."* Psalms 89:37

"For thy mercy is great above the heavens: and thy truth <u>reacheth unto the clouds</u>." Psalms 108:4

"By his knowledge the depths are broken up, and <u>the clouds</u> drop down the dew." Proverbs 3:20

"When he established <u>the clouds</u> above: when he strengthened the fountains of the deep:" Proverbs 8:28

"Behold, the nations are as a drop of a bucket, and are counted <u>as the small dust</u> of the balance: behold, he taketh up the isles as a very little thing." Isaiah 40:15

"Drop down, ye heavens, from above, and <u>let the skies</u> pour down righteousness: let the earth open, and let them bring forth salvation, and let righteousness spring up together; I the LORD have created it." Isaiah 45:8

"We would have healed Babylon, but she is not healed: forsake her, and let us go every one into his own country: for her judgment reacheth unto heaven, and is lifted up <u>even to the skies</u>." Jeremiah 51:9

Do these Scriptures describe a glass dome? No, most of them are pointing to the *clouds* in the *sky*. By that we see that Job 37:18 is pointing to the sky in which the clouds move, not to a glass dome.

The Strong's Hebrew for *"glass"* is 7209 *r@'iy*; which means: *a mirror — a looking glass.*

They didn't have glass mirrors in Job's day, so they beat metal into sheets and polished it, to be able to see their reflection. The Greek Septuagint Bible translates it as *"Wilt thou establish with him foundations for the ancient heavens? they are strong as a molten mirror."*

The English Standard Version Bible translates it as *"Can you, like him, spread out the skies, hard as a cast metal mirror?"*

It's declaring the glory of a clear night sky, which allows you to see the many distant stars in the expanse of the heavens, reflecting the glory of Yahuah's creation. Job 37:18 is not proof of a flat earth dome, just more proof that it's the sky, the heavens, which are *spread out*.

Psalms 19:1 *"The heavens declare the glory of God; and the firmament sheweth his handiwork."*

Nathan says: A man who is determined to undermine the scriptural proof of the firmament undermines the handywork of Yahweh.

The verses that Nathan cites have not proven that the firmament is a glass dome, so his accusation is without merit.

In Psalms 19:1-6, David describes the sun traveling in a *circuit*, through the constellations, proclaiming the Gospel. *"The heavens declare the glory of God; and the firmament sheweth his handywork. Day unto day uttereth speech, and night unto night sheweth knowledge. There is no speech nor language, where their voice is not heard. Their line is gone out through all the earth, and their words to the end of the world. In them hath he set a tabernacle for the sun, which is as a bridegroom <u>coming out of his chamber</u>, and rejoiceth <u>as a strong man to run a race</u>. <u>His going forth</u> is from the end of the heaven, and <u>his circuit</u> unto the ends of it: and there is nothing hid from the heat thereof."*

We can see that Yahuah is referring to the *circle* of the mazzaroth, which acts as a constant witness to those on earth, about His great power, and His redemption plan. This is the same *circle* that is described in Isaiah 40:22, which is not pointing to the earth itself, but to the *ecliptic circle* that surrounds the globe earth.

Once again the word *firmament* is not pointing to a glass dome, but to the *expanse of the heavens*, in which the sun and constellations witness about His handiwork.

Psalms 19:1-6 describes a geocentric universe, as the sun is *going forth* and *running a race* through the constellations on the *circuit* of the ecliptic line which surrounds the globe earth.

Psalms 150:1 *"Praise ye the LORD. Praise God in his sanctuary: praise him in the firmament of his power."*

The word *"firmament"* in this verse is not pointing to the design of the earth; it's pointing to the vast *expanse* of Yahuah's power. The KJ3 Literal Translation Bible reads, *"Praise Jehovah! Praise God in His holy place; praise Him in the expanse of His might."*

The whole chapter is about praising Yahuah, not about a glass dome. *"Praise him for his mighty acts: praise him according to his excellent greatness. Praise him with the sound of the trumpet: praise him with the psaltery and harp. Praise him with the timbrel and dance: praise him with stringed instruments and organs. Praise him upon the loud cymbals: praise him upon the high sounding cymbals. Let every thing that hath breath praise the LORD. Praise ye the LORD."* Psalms 150:2-6

Nathan *cherry-picked* this verse without understanding the context. Flat-earthers, how do you defend this verse being on the list?

Proverbs 8:28 *"When he established the clouds above: when he strengthened the fountains of the deep."*

I'm not clear on why Nathan listed this verse as a proof of the supposed glass dome over the flat earth. It may be because the Hebrew word for *"clouds"* is 7834 *shachaq; a powder (as beaten small): by analogy, a thin vapor; by extension, the firmament:—cloud, small dust, heaven, sky.*

It's the same word that's used in Job 37:18 as *sky*, *"Hast thou with him spread out the sky, which is strong, and as a molten looking glass?"* In my explanation of Job 37:18, I listed many verses which use the word *shachaq*, and none of them pointed to a dome, and most of them pointed to *clouds* which are in the *expanse of the heavens*.

Yahuah established the clouds in the sky, and He established the waters under the earth. It's saying that the clouds are part of the *firmament*, the *heaven*, the *sky*; which again shows that the firmament is not a glass dome.

Isaiah 40:22 *"It is he who sits above the circle of the earth, And its inhabitants are like grasshoppers; Who stretches out the heavens like a curtain, And spreads them out like a tent to dwell in."*

Nathan says: This verse shares the same language as Job 26:7. What in the "heavens" is being "stretched out" as a curtain? What in the "heavens" are "spread out that would allow us to live under it as a "tent?"

I addressed this in the *Earth is a Disk/Circle* section. It's pointing to the ecliptic *circle* which surrounds the globe earth; not a circular flat earth. Yahuah is not sitting on the earth but in the heavens.

Nathan's question is ironic, as the answer is in his question, for many verses declare that it's the *heavens* which are *stretched out*, not a glass dome. How is he missing this clear point?

When you're in a *tent*, you're surrounded by it. The same is true about the *expanse of heavens*, the planisphere, which surrounds the globe earth. Isaiah 40:22 points to a globe earth, not a flat earth.

Isaiah 42:5 *"Thus saith God the LORD, he that created the heavens, and stretched them out; he that spread forth the earth, and that which cometh out of it; he that giveth breath unto the people upon it, and spirit to them that walk therein:"*

It says that the heavens are *stretched out* and that the earth is *spread forth* (*raqa*), not a glass dome. Nathan's explanations are *stretching* the truth as he's forcing an explanation onto the text that isn't there.

Isaiah 44:24 *"Thus saith the LORD, thy redeemer, and he that formed thee from the womb, I am the LORD that maketh all things; that stretcheth forth (natah) the heavens alone; that spreadeth abroad (raqa) the earth by myself;"*

Once again, this verse is proclaiming that the *heavens* are stretched forth, not a glass dome. *"Stretched forth"* is Strong's Hebrew word 5186 *natah*; which means *to stretch or spread out, to bend away*. Are the heavens around the globe earth not *stretched out, spread out,* to bend around the earth? Yes, so it's not a flat-earth proof.

Isaiah 45:12 *"I have made the earth, and created man upon it: I, even my hands, have stretched out the heavens, and all their host have I commanded."*

Nathan adds: This verse, Isaiah 45:12, is in agreement with Job 26:7 and Job 37:18, as well as, there is no contradiction within the inspired words of Yahuah. Only a fool is willing to declare Yahuah a liar by stating that His hands have NOT stretched out the heavens. *"Let Yahuah be true and every man a liar."* **Romans 3:4**

Job 26:7 and Job 37:18 didn't prove that the earth is flat with a dome over it, so his point is without merit. I don't understand Nathan's logic. *"The heavens"* are the expanse where the *host*, the stars, were placed during creation. It's describing the expanse of the heavens that is stretched out, not a glass dome.

The Hebrew word *"shamayim"* is describing the *sky*, in which the stars dwell and clouds move; not a glass dome. Isaiah 51:13 gives a similar message, that the heavens were stretched forth, *"And forgettest the LORD thy maker, that hath stretched forth the heavens, and laid the foundations of the earth."*

Zechariah 12:1 reinforces it, *"The burden of the word of the LORD for Israel, saith the LORD, which stretcheth forth the heavens, and layeth the foundation of the earth, and formeth the spirit of man within him."*

Once again, Nathan is intermixing terms, by proclaiming that *"Only a fool is willing to declare Yahuah a liar by stating that His hands have NOT stretched out the heavens."*

He's implying that the *"heavens"* are the glass dome, but the Hebrew words are not the same. Only a fool can't see that Scripture repeatedly declares that it's the *expanse of heavens that are stretched* out, not a glass dome.

Isaiah 48:13 *"Mine hand also hath laid the foundation of the earth, and my right hand hath spanned the heavens: when I call unto them, they stand up together."*

Nathan adds: What is being 'spanned' by Yahuah in the heavens?

It's not saying that Yahuah spanned the heavens *with* something, such as a glass dome, as Nathan is implying. The Strong's Hebrew word for "spanned" is 2946 *taphach;* which means *to flatten out or extend (as a tent); figuratively, to nurse a child (as promotive of growth); from dandling on the palms:—span, swaddle.*

It's saying that Yahuah *extended* out the expanse of heavens during creation, by the power of His mighty hand. The celestial sphere of stars in heaven obeyed His commands at creation to be positioned at exacting places in the planisphere.

Ezekiel 1:22-26 *"And the likeness of the firmament upon the heads of the living creature was as the color of the terrible crystal, stretched forth over their heads above. And under the firmament were their wings straight, the one toward the other: every one had two, which covered on this side, and every one had two, which covered on that side, their bodies. And when they went, I heard the noise of their wings, like the noise of great waters, as the voice of the Almighty, the voice of speech, as the noise of an host: when they stood, they let down their wings. And there was a voice from the firmament that was over their heads, when they stood, and had let down their wings. And above the firmament that was over their heads was the likeness of a throne, as the appearance of a sapphire stone: and upon the likeness of the throne was the likeness as the appearance of a man above upon it."*

Nathan adds: The analogies of the "firmament" make no sense without a literal "firmament."

Nathan is making a false association, for nowhere in Scripture does it say that an analogy has to have a literal fulfillment somewhere else. Do we believe that there's a glass dome above Yahuah's head? No!

The Strong's Hebrew word for *"crystal"* is 7140 *qerach*; which means *ice (as if bald, i.e., smooth); hence, hail; by resemblance, rock crystal:— crystal, frost, ice.* The ice crystals seem to reflect the brightness of Yahuah, which causes the rainbow.

Revelation 4:3 points to a rainbow above His throne, *"And he that sat was to look upon like a jasper and a sardine stone: and there was a rainbow round about the throne, in sight like unto an emerald."*

Revelation 10:1 also says rainbow, *"And I saw another mighty angel come down from heaven, clothed with a cloud: and a rainbow was upon his head, and his face was as it were the sun, and his feet as pillars of fire:"*

Does it not make more sense that there's an *expanse* above our Heavenly Father's head, in which the colors of a rainbow appear? Nathan's false association doesn't prove that there's a glass dome over a flat earth.

Ezekiel 10:1 *"Then I looked, and, behold, in the firmament that was above the head of the cherubims there appeared over them as it were a sapphire stone, as the appearance of the likeness of a throne."*

Are we to believe that there's a glass dome above the heaven where Yahuah dwells? No! It's speaking about an expanse which is above the head of the cherubims, in the chambers of heaven where Yahuah dwells.

Interestingly, we've seen how the throne is above the north celestial pole star. Below it is a planisphere of constellations which surround the globe earth as a curtain, but above it, above Yahuah's throne, there is a vast expanse.

Daniel 12:3 *"And they that be wise shall shine as the brightness of the firmament; and they that turn many to righteousness as the stars for ever and ever."*

Are we to believe that a flat earth dome has brightness? No! This verse is telling us what the firmament (*raqiya*) is, as it points to the bright, shining stars in the *expanse of heaven*! The saints are portrayed as *stars*, which *shine* in the heaven of our Creator.

I'm amazed that Nathan cherry-picks verses just because they use the word *"firmament"* without understanding the proper context. I'm even more amazed that people promote his 'flat earth Bible verse list.'

Amos 9:6 *"It is he that buildeth his stories in the heaven, and hath founded his troop in the earth; he that calleth for the waters of the* *sea, and poureth them out upon the face of the earth: The LORD is his name."*

Nathan adds: Some translations use the word "troop." Have you researched the original Hebrew meaning of that word? "Strong's 92 OT (Hebrew 'aguddahag-ood-daw' feminine passive participle of an unused root (meaning to bind); a band, bundle, knot, or arch:–bunch, burden, troop." Did you see the word "arch" in there? Again, no inconsistency in God's Word.

The word *"stories"* is pointing to the *elevation* of heaven, once again pointing to how the *expanse of heaven*, the *firmament*, is stretched out.

The Septuagint, the Greek Old Testament, has a completely different reading, *"It is he that builds up to the sky, and established his promise on earth; who calls the water of the sea, and pours it out on the face of the earth; the Lord Almighty is his name."*

The 1587 Geneva Bible reads, *"He buildeth his spheres in the heauen, and hath layde the foundation of his globe of elementes in the earth: hee calleth the waters of the sea, and powreth them out vpon the open earth: the Lorde is his Name."*

This image shows the *"stories,"* the spheres of heaven. Each sphere serves a different purpose, to protect life on earth.

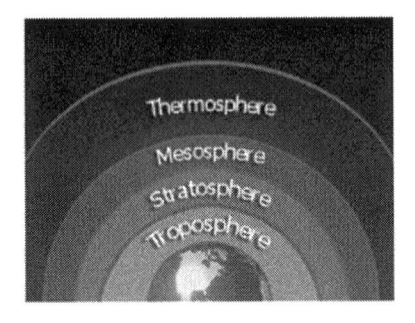

The Troposphere is the lowest part of the atmosphere which contains our weather - clouds, rain, snow. The Stratosphere contains much of the ozone which protects us.

I'm not clear how Nathan proclaiming that the word *"troop"* doesn't mean an *arch*, is proving that there's a glass dome over the flat earth. It says that the *"troop"* is *"in"* the earth, not *over* the earth. It's pointing to the *band* or *knot* that binds the fountains of the deep.

Amos 9:6 matches the narrative in Psalms 33:7, *"He gathereth the waters of the sea together as an heap: he layeth up the depth in storehouses."* It matches the narrative in Job 38:8, *"Or who shut up the sea with doors, when it brake forth, as if it had issued out of the womb?"*

And it matches the narrative in Psalms 104:5-9, which says that the deep waters are bound, *"Who laid the foundations of the earth, that it should not be removed for ever. Thou coveredst it with the deep as with a garment: the waters stood above the mountains. At thy rebuke they fled; at the voice of thy thunder they hasted away. They go up by the mountains; they go down by the valleys unto the place which thou hast founded for them. Thou hast set a bound that they may not pass over; that they turn not again to cover the earth."*

Amos 9:6 does not prove that the earth is flat with a dome over it, and it seems to point to arched spheres which surround the globe earth, and to the circular layers under the globe earth which bind the fountains of the deep.

Acts 7:56 *"And said, Behold, I see the heavens opened, and the Son of man standing on the right hand of God."*

Nathan adds: If the "heavens" are only the open expanse/sky, why would it have to be re-opened? What is being "opened?" Perhaps, the firmament?

Why would a glass dome have to be opened to see the Son of Man?

The word *"heavens"* is Strong's Greek 3772. *Ouranos,* which means *the sky; by extension, heaven (as the abode of God); by implication, happiness, power, eternity; especially, the Gospel:—air, heaven(-ly), sky.*

It's a different word than *firmament*, which Nathan claims is a glass dome. There's a lack of integrity here, as Nathan is intermixing the words *'heaven'* and *'firmament.'* But this verse is not saying that a supposed glass dome firmament was opened, just the heavens; so it's not a flat earth proof.

Revelation 4:6 *"And before the throne there was a sea of glass like unto crystal: and in the midst of the throne, and round about the throne, were four beasts full of eyes before and behind."*

Nathan cites it because it uses the phrase *"glass like unto crystal,"* but it's not describing a glass dome; and Scripture has declared that the *firmament is the expanse of heaven.*

Revelation 6:14 *"And the heaven departed as a scroll when it is rolled together, and every mountain and island were moved out of their places."*

Nathan says: What is being "departed as a scroll when it is rolled together?" If anyone is causing a divide/wedge over the true existence of the dome/firmament it is the obstinance of the man's refusal to accept God's Word for His firmament.

The verse says that *"heaven"* will depart as a scroll, not a glass dome. Revelation 6:12-14 point to the sun, moon, and stars; which are in the *expanse of heaven.* It's Nathan who is obstinate in refusing to see the clear explanation.

A glass dome firmament is one of the major concepts of flat-earthers, but the verses that Nathan cites prove that the firmament is the *expanse of heaven.* This confirms the definition which is given in Genesis 1:8, *"And God called the firmament Heaven."*

CHAPTER 27

Sun Moves, not the Earth

Nathan cites Genesis 15:12, Genesis 15:17, Genesis 19:23, Genesis 32:31, Exodus 17:12, Exodus 22:3, Exodus 22:26, Leviticus 22:7, Numbers 2:3, Numbers 21:11, Numbers 34:15, Deuteronomy 4:41, Deuteronomy 4:47, Deuteronomy 11:30, Deuteronomy 16:6, Deuteronomy 23:11, Deuteronomy 24:13, Deuteronomy 24:15, Joshua 1:15, Joshua 8:29, Joshua 10:27, Joshua 12:1, Joshua 13:5, Joshua 19:12, Joshua 19:27, Joshua 19:34, Judges 8:13, Judges 9:33, Judges 14:18, Judges 19:14, Judges 20:43, 2 Samuel 2:24, 2 Samuel 3:35, 2 Samuel 23:4, 1 Kings 22:36, 2 Chronicles 18:34, Psalm 50:1, Psalm 113:3, Ecclesiastes 1:5, Isaiah 41:25, Isaiah 45:6, Isaiah 59:19, Jeremiah 15:9, Daniel 6:14, Amos 8:9, Jonah 4:8, Micah 3:6, Nahum 3:17, Malachi 1:11, Matthew 5:45, Mark 16:2, Ephesians 4:26, James 1:11

Nathan notes: The Bible uses words that describe the sun, with only a few known exceptions, as "moving," though some believe that words like "rising" and "down" imply the sun is moving "up" and "down" over the alleged curvature of the earth. In addition to spinning globe earth believing Christians completely missing the fact that the Bible uses words which describe the sun as "moving" they also fail to analyze the original Hebrew and Greek meaning of those same words.

The original Hebrew and Greek words have meanings, such as, to come, to go, to irradiate (or shoot forth beams), to appear, as soon as it appears, eastside, eastward, an entrance, the west, by which came, as cometh, in coming, entering, entrance into, entry, where goeth, westward.

And, these words are relating to the placement ("direction") of the sun in relation to the context of the particular Biblical account.

Unless one is willing to depart from the true meanings of these words and cause contradictions with other verses that state the earth as being FLAT, there is no case to be made for the sun to be "rising or "going down" over the alleged curvature of the imaginary and unprovable ball/sphere shaped earth. To research the original Hebrew and Greek of the words in any of the verses referenced on this webpage there are many good online resources, including, Bible Hub and Restoration Study Bible.

I won't bore you by listing all of these verses. You can look them up if you like. Nathan's argument in this section is against the heliocentric globe earth model. He cites them to proclaim that the sun is moving. They use words such as; *arise, raiseth, arose, down, go down, going down, gone down, riseth, risen, riseth not, rising, rose, sunrising, up, went down.*

Now ask yourself, does the sun do any of those things on the flat earth model? Does it literally rise? Does it literally go down? No, so citing them to proclaim that they're flat-earth verses is either ignorant or deception.

If those terms are *symbolic* and referring to our viewpoint, as the sun seems to rise and go down; that can apply to the flat earth model, the heliocentric globe earth model, and the geocentric globe earth model.

If those terms are *literal*, then they don't apply to the flat earth model or the heliocentric globe earth model; and they fit perfectly with the geocentric globe earth model.

Nathan citing these verses to proclaim that they prove that the earth is flat reveals his intellectual dishonesty.

CHAPTER 28

Sun STOPS moving

Nathan cites Isaiah 60:20, Job 9:7, Joshua 10:12-14, Habakkuk 3:11

He points to these passages which say that the sun was stopped, to proclaim that it doesn't fit the heliocentric globe earth model; and then he asks *"If you believe God's Word to be Faithful and true, what other explanation do you have?"* It amazes me that he asks this question, as it's possible for the sun to be stopped in a geocentric globe-earth universe.

Isaiah 60:20 *"Thy sun shall no more go down; neither shall thy moon withdraw itself: for the LORD shall be thine everlasting light, and the days of thy mourning shall be ended."*

The context of the verse shows that it's using poetic language to point to the promised Messiah, and a time when there will be no sun or moon, when we are with our Father and Messiah.

The previous verse says, *"The sun shall be no more thy light by day; neither for brightness shall the moon give light unto thee: but the LORD shall be unto thee an everlasting light, and thy God thy glory."* Isaiah 60:19

The Jews mourned while they were in Babylonian captivity, but Isaiah promised the set-apart ones that there would come a time when there will be no more tears. *"And God shall wipe away all tears from their eyes; and there shall be no more death, neither sorrow, nor crying, neither shall there be any more pain: for the former things are passed away."* Revelation 21:4

Revelation 21:23 points to this time, *"And the city had no need of the sun, neither of the moon, to shine in it: for the glory of God did lighten it, and the Lamb is the light thereof."*

Revelation 22:5 also points to this time, *"And there shall be no night there; and they need no candle, neither light of the sun; for the Lord God giveth them light: and they shall reign for ever and ever."* HalleluYah!

Isaiah 60:20 isn't talking about the sun being stopped, it's pointing to a time when there won't be a sun, so it's not a flat earth proof.

Job 9:7 *"Which commandeth the sun, and it riseth not; and sealeth up the stars."*

The previous verses talk about mountains being removed and the earth shaken out of its place. This verse follows the same pattern in talking about an event that's not normal.

It's not talking about our view of the sun rising, but rather it's a direct command to the sun to stop moving. This is contrary to the heliocentric model, but it can apply to the flat earth model or the geocentric globe earth model, so it's not a flat earth proof.

Joshua 10:12-14 *"Then spake Joshua to the LORD in the day when the LORD delivered up the Amorites before the children of Israel, and he said in the sight of Israel, Sun, stand thou still upon Gibeon; and thou, Moon, in the valley of Ajalon. And the sun stood still, and the moon stayed, until the people had avenged themselves upon their enemies. Is not this written in the book of Jasher? So the sun stood still in the midst of heaven, and hasted not to go down about a whole day. And there was no day like that before it or after it, that the LORD hearkened unto the voice of a man: for the LORD fought for Israel."*

Proclaiming that the sun stood still tells us that it's an unusual occurrence; as the sun normally is not standing still. It says that on no other day, before it or after it, has the sun stood still like this. It's a valid argument against the heliocentric model, as the sun doesn't move.

People who defend the heliocentric model have to make excuses to dismiss the plain language. Since it also fits the geocentric globe earth universe model, it's not a flat earth proof.

Habakkuk 3:11 *"The sun and moon stood still in their habitation: at the light of thine arrows they went, and at the shining of thy glittering spear."*

Nathan lists it because it doesn't make sense on the heliocentric globe earth model, as the sun always stands still. It declares that both the sun and moon stood still, indicating that they both are normally moving.

This is another solid proof that the Bible is proclaiming that the sun is moving, and people who defend the heliocentric model have to make excuses to dismiss the clear language.

When you read the verses in this and the previous chapter, they match up with a geocentric globe earth universe without any contradictions.

This section shows Nathan's lack of integrity, as a geocentric universe also fits the description, but he doesn't mention it. A fair discussion about the shape of the earth and design of the universe should include the geocentric globe earth as an option.

"But thanks be to God, which giveth us the victory through our Lord Jesus Christ. Therefore, my beloved brethren, be ye stedfast, unmoveable, always abounding in the work of the Lord, forasmuch as ye know that your labour is not in vain in the Lord."
1 Corinthians 15-57-58

CHAPTER 29

Sun moves BACKWARDS

Nathan cites 2 Kings 20:8-11 *"And Hezekiah said unto Isaiah, What shall be the sign that the LORD will heal me, and that I shall go up into the house of the LORD the third day? And Isaiah said, This sign shalt thou have of the LORD, that the LORD will do the thing that he hath spoken: shall the shadow go forward ten degrees, or go back ten degrees? And Hezekiah answered, It is a light thing for the shadow to go down ten degrees: nay, but let the shadow return backward ten degrees. And Isaiah the prophet cried unto the LORD: and he brought the shadow ten degrees backward, by which it had gone down in the dial of Ahaz."*

Notice that the verse doesn't say that the sun was moved, but that the shadow of the sun was moved backward. On the heliocentric globe earth model, that could happen by moving the earth back, so the verses that Nathan cites doesn't prove anything.

The context is that King Hezekiah is sick and near death. *"In those days was Hezekiah sick unto death. And the prophet Isaiah the son of Amoz came to him, and said unto him, Thus saith the LORD, Set thine house in order; for thou shalt die, and not live."* 2 Kings 20:1

But because of his repentance, a sign was given that his life would be extended. *"Turn again, and tell Hezekiah the captain of my people, Thus saith the LORD, the God of David thy father, I have heard thy prayer, I have seen thy tears: behold, I will heal thee: on the third day thou shalt go up unto the house of the LORD. And I will add unto thy days fifteen years; and I will deliver thee and this city out of the hand of the king of Assyria; and I will defend this city for mine own sake, and for my servant David's sake."* 2 Kings 20:5-6

2 Chronicles 32 records the same time when Hezekiah was sick. *"In those days Hezekiah was sick to the death, and prayed unto the LORD: and he spake unto him, and he gave him a sign. But Hezekiah rendered not again according to the benefit done unto him; for his heart was lifted up: therefore there was wrath upon him, and upon Judah and Jerusalem. Notwithstanding Hezekiah humbled himself for the pride of his heart, both he and the inhabitants of Jerusalem, so that the wrath of the LORD came not upon them in the days of Hezekiah."* 2 Chronicles 32:24-26

Isaiah 38 points to the same timeframe and it says that it is the sun which was moved back ten degrees: *"And this shall be a sign unto thee from the LORD, that the LORD will do this thing that he hath spoken; Behold, I will bring again the shadow of the degrees, which is gone down in the sun dial of Ahaz, ten degrees backward. So the sun returned ten degrees, by which degrees it was gone down."* Isaiah 38:7-8

Now that we have proof that it was the sun that was moved backward, returned ten degrees; we can make proper conclusions.

If the earth was moved back to make this happen, then the text would say that *the earth was returned*.

If the sun is the center of the universe, it's not possible to move it so that it causes the shadow on earth to move back ten degrees, so that is contrary to the heliocentric globe earth model.

If the sun was moved back to create one long day, then it could have been moved back on a flat earth model or the geocentric globe earth model, so it's not a flat earth proof.

"As soon then as he had said unto them, I am he, they went backward, and fell to the ground."
John 18:6

CHAPTER 30

Moon has its own Light

Nathan cites Genesis 1:16, Isaiah 13:10, Isaiah 30:26, Isaiah 60:19-20, Jeremiah 31:35, Ezekiel 32:7, Matthew 24:29, Mark 13:24, Revelation 21:23

Flat-earthers have to dismiss that the sun illuminates the moon because it causes problems on their model. For example, at night when the moon is overhead, and the sun is on the opposite side of the flat earth; how would the sun's rays strike the moon to illuminate it, but not illuminate the sky around it?

Genesis 1:16 *"And God made two great lights; the greater light to rule the day, and the lesser light to rule the night: he made the stars also."*

Nathan says that *"to light"* **in Genesis 1:17 literally means that the moon itself gives light – there is no way out of this meaning!** *"And God set them in the firmament of the heaven to give light upon the earth."*

The Hebrew verb for *"to give light"* is 215 *'owr*; which means *to be (causative, make)* luminous *(literally and metaphorically):— break of day, glorious, kindle, (be, en-, give, show) light (-en, -ened), set on fire, shine.*

That definition does not proclaim that the moon gives its own light. It says that the light can be a *luminous body*.

Isaiah 60:1 gives an example of how *light shines* (*'owr*), as we're called to shine in the glory of Yahuah. *"Arise, shine; for thy light is come, and the glory of the LORD is risen upon thee."*

The words *"for thy light"* is Hebrew noun 216 *owr*; which means illumination or luminary: *bright, clear, day, light morning, sun.*

The Hebrew word for *"lights"* in Genesis 1:16 is 3974 *ma'owr*; which means, *a luminous body or luminary, i.e. (abstractly) light (as an element): figuratively, brightness; specifically, a chandelier:—bright, light.*

The KJ3 Literal Translation Bible uses the word *"luminary"* instead of *"light"*: *"And God made the two great luminaries: the great luminary to rule the day, and the small luminary and the stars to rule the night. And God set them in the expanse of the heavens, to give light on the earth, and to rule over the day and over the night; and to divide between the light and between the darkness. And God saw that it was good."*

Genesis 1:14-15 in the KJ3 Literal Translation Bible uses the word luminary. *"And God said, let luminaries in the expanse of the heavens, to divide between the day and between the night. And let them be for signs and for seasons, and for days and years. And let them be for luminaries in the expanse of heavens, to give light on the earth. And it was so."*

Scripture is saying that the moon can provide light by being a luminous body which reflects the sun's light.

Isaiah 13:10 *"For the stars of heaven and the constellations thereof shall not give their light: the sun shall be darkened in his going forth, and the moon shall not cause her light to shine."*

Rob Skiba proclaims, *"What? The stars and constellations are all going to "wink out" and no longer give their light? But what about the alleged planets going around those stars? Of course, we can try and rationalize this away and say that we just won't be able to see them because the sky on Earth is going to be cloudy or offer up some other lame, eisegetical explanation, but that's not what the text says."*

The verse is not pointing to the physical *sun, moon, and stars*; rather, it's symbolically pointing to the overthrow of the Babylonian kingdom. Heavenly bodies can be used symbolically to describe earthly dignitaries and great political authorities.

Genesis 37:8-10 gives us a great example of how the heavenly bodies can symbolize leadership organization. Joseph had a dream, which he shared with his family. *"And this time, the sun, the moon, and the eleven stars bowed down to me. So he told it to his father and his brothers; and his father rebuked him and said to him, "What is this dream that you have dreamed? Shall your mother and I and your brothers indeed come to bow down to the earth before you?"*

Joseph's father understood that he was symbolized by the sun, and was disturbed by the thought that he (sun), his wife (moon) and his eleven other sons (stars) would bow down before Joseph.

Isaiah 13:10 is referring to the Babylonians (the king is the *sun*, the queen is the *moon*, and the leaders are the *stars*) being removed from power by the Medo-Persians. Isaiah 13:17 confirms this with, *"Behold, I will stir up the Medes against them."*

Isaiah 13:10 is not referring to the physical moon, so it's not proof that the moon illuminates itself.

Isaiah 30:26 *"Moreover the light of the moon shall be as the light of the sun, and the light of the sun shall be sevenfold, as the light of seven days, in the day that the LORD bindeth up the breach of his people, and healeth the stroke of their wound."*

First of all, it's declaring that *the light of the moon shall be as the light of the sun*. If the sun is sevenfold brighter, then the moon shines sevenfold brighter, which demonstrates their direct relationship.

Secondly, this verse is not speaking literally, but is a hyperbolical expression of the most glorious condition of Yahuah's assembly of saints, far surpassing what it was in former ages. Messiah is our *Sun of Righteousness*, our High Priest; who is far superior to the Israelite High Priest.

Messiah said that the saints are the light of the world who *reflect* His love and Gospel message, *"Ye are the light of the world. A city that is set on an hill cannot be hid. Neither do men light a candle, and put it under a bushel, but on a candlestick; and it giveth light unto all that are in the house. Let your light so shine before men, that they may see your good works, and glorify your Father which is in heaven."* Matthew 5:14-16

"Then shall the righteous shine forth as the sun in the kingdom of their Father. Who hath ears to hear, let him hear." Matthew 13:43

"For God, who commanded the light to shine out of darkness, hath shined in our hearts, to give the light of the knowledge of the glory of God in the face of Jesus Christ." 2 Corinthians 4:6

"That ye may be blameless and harmless, the sons of God, without rebuke, in the midst of a crooked and perverse nation, among whom ye shine as lights in the world." Philippians 2:15

The saints *shine* because they reflect the *light* of the Son. It's using metaphoric language, and it's not about the real moon, so it's not a flat-earth proof.

Isaiah 60:19-20 *"The sun shall be no more thy light by day; neither for brightness shall the moon give light unto thee: but the LORD shall be unto thee an everlasting light, and thy God thy glory. Thy sun shall no more go down; neither shall thy moon withdraw itself: for the LORD shall be thine everlasting light, and the days of thy mourning shall be ended."*

These verses are foretelling the day when the Father and Son will illuminate the New Jerusalem. Revelation 21:23 points to this time, *"And the city had no need of the sun, neither of the moon, to shine in it: for the glory of God did lighten it, and the Lamb is the light thereof."* Revelation 22:5 also points to this time, *"And there shall be no night there; and they need no candle, neither light of the sun; for the Lord God giveth them light: and they shall reign for ever and ever."*

These verses do not declare that the moon has its own light, and since this is about New Jerusalem, where there is no moon; it's not a flat earth proof.

Jeremiah 31:35 *"Thus saith the LORD, which giveth the sun for a light by day, and the ordinances of the moon and of the stars for a light by night, which divideth the sea when the waves thereof roar; The LORD of hosts is his name:"*

This verse does not declare that the moon has its own light. Nathan believes that to be true, so he presses it onto the verse, but the Hebrew word for light can point to a *luminous body or luminary*.

Ezekiel 32:7 *"And when I shall put thee out, I will cover the heaven, and make the stars thereof dark; I will cover the sun with a cloud, and the moon shall not give her light."*

It does not say that He would cover the moon, just the sun. It says that He will cover the sun, and the moon will not give its light; so we see the direct relationship. It proves that the sun illuminates the moon, which is the opposite of what Nathan is claiming.

But the context of this verse is not talking about the physical sun and moon. It's symbolically speaking about the kingdom of Egypt, which Yahuah was judging by sending armies against it; so that the king (*sun*), the queen or priesthood (*moon*), and the nobles, princes, counselors, etc. (*stars*) were darkened; removed from power.

Matthew 24:29 *"Immediately after the tribulation of those days shall the sun be darkened, and the moon shall not give her light, and the stars shall fall from heaven, and the powers of the heavens shall be shaken."*

Mark 13:24 *"But in those days, after that tribulation, the sun shall be darkened, and the moon shall not give her light."*

Both of these verses are about prophecy fulfillment, so they're not referring to normal circumstances on the earth. The text does not say that the moon has its own light, so it's not a flat-earth proof text. If anything, the verses imply that because the sun is darkened, then the moon will not give its light; which once again shows their direct relationship.

Because they're prophetic verses, they can symbolically be pointing to an evil leadership system being removed from power. An example of this is the Jewish leadership system which rejected their promised Messiah and delivered Him up to be killed, whom He called *"serpents, a generation of vipers."*

In 70 AD, the High Priest (*sun*), Sanhedrin (*moon*) and priests (*stars*) were all either killed or captured and sold as slaves; so that the Jewish leadership was darkened. And their temple was desolated.

Revelation 21:23 *"And the city had no need of the sun, neither of the moon, to shine in it: for the glory of God did lighten it, and the Lamb is the light thereof."*

How does this prove that the moon has its own light? It's saying that there's no need for the sun or moon in the New Jerusalem. Flat-earthers, how do you defend these verses being on the list?

"This then is the message which we have heard of him, and declare unto you, that God is light, and in him is no darkness at all. If we say that we have fellowship with him, and walk in darkness, we lie, and do not the truth: But if we walk in the light, as he is in the light, we have fellowship one with another, and the blood of Jesus Christ his Son cleanseth us from all sin."
1 John 1:5-7

CHAPTER 31

High Altitude Perspectives

Nathan cites Daniel 4:11, Daniel 4:20, Matthew 4:8

Daniel 4:11 *"The tree grew, and was strong, and the height thereof reached unto heaven, and the sight thereof to the end of all the earth:"*

Flat-earthers proclaim that this giant tree is only possible on a flat earth. First of all, everyone on the flat earth can't see the North Star, so how would they see a giant tree? Secondly, the location of the tree is in Babylon, not at the center of a flat earth.

But this verse isn't even talking about a real tree, as its part of a dream. The tree symbolizes King Nebuchadnezzar of Babylon, who reigned over the kingdoms of the earth. He was cut down, humbled and made to eat grass like the cattle of the field for seven years. This is just another example of Nathan Roberts taking a verse completely out of context to try to prove his beliefs.

Daniel 4:20 *"The tree that thou sawest, which grew, and was strong, whose height reached unto the heaven, and the sight thereof to all the earth."*

How flat-earthers don't bother to read the rest of the chapter, I cannot understand; or if they do, how do they ignore the clear explanation?

Verse 22 tells us that the tree represents King Nebuchadnezzar. *"It is thou, O king, that art grown and become strong; for thy greatness is grown, and reacheth unto heaven, and thy dominion to the end of the earth."*

Let's read how he was humbled and then praised His Creator. *"The same hour was the thing fulfilled upon Nebuchadnezzar: and he was driven from men, and did eat grass as oxen, and his body was wet with the dew of heaven, till his hairs were grown like eagles' feathers, and his nails like birds' claws. And at the end of the days I Nebuchadnezzar lifted up mine eyes unto heaven, and mine understanding returned unto me, and I blessed the most High, and I praised and honoured him that liveth for ever, whose dominion is an everlasting dominion, and his kingdom is from generation to generation: At the same time my reason returned unto me; and for the glory of my kingdom, mine honour and brightness returned unto me; and my counsellers and my lords sought unto me; and I was established in my kingdom, and excellent majesty was added unto me. Now I Nebuchadnezzar praise and extol and honor the King of heaven, all whose works are truth, and his ways judgment: and those that walk in pride he is able to abase."* Daniel 2:33-37. HalleluYah!

Neither Daniel 4:11 or 4:20 is a flat earth proof. Listing them shows that Nathan fails to understand, or blatantly ignores, the proper context of Scripture to promote his beliefs.

Matthew 4:8 *"Again, the devil taketh him up into an exceeding high mountain, and sheweth him all the kingdoms of the world, and the glory of them;"*

Can you see Mount Everest from where you live? No, so it's ridiculous to proclaim that this is a flat earth proof. The devil may have been pointing to that region of the world, Judea and the surrounding nations. Or he was able to give a visual representation of all of the nations of the world.

Either way, there is no mountain on Earth from which you can see all of the kingdoms of the world. Flat-earthers, how do you defend these verses being on the list?

CHAPTER 32

Hell is a bottomless pit at the heart of the [flat disc] earth

Nathan cites Revelation 9:1-2, 11, Revelation 11:7, Revelation 17:8, Revelation 20:1, Revelation 20:3

Revelation 9:1-2 *"And the fifth angel sounded, and I saw a star fall from heaven unto the earth: and to him was given the key of the bottomless pit. And he opened the bottomless pit; and there arose a smoke out of the pit, as the smoke of a great furnace; and the sun and the air were darkened by reason of the smoke of the pit."*

Nathan seems to be implying that only a flat-earth can have a bottomless pit, as the depth of a globe earth is limited; but the Greek word describes an *abyss*, a *deep pit*. That can exist on a flat earth or globe earth, so it's not a flat earth proof.

The KJ3 Literal Translation Bible reads, *"And the fifth angel sounded his trumpet. And I saw a star out of the heaven falling onto the earth. And the key to the pit of the abyss was given to it. And he opened the pit of the abyss. And smoke went up out of the pit, like smoke of a great furnace. And the sun was darkened, and the air, by the smoke of the pit."*

The fifth trumpet of Revelation is a prophetic vision which uses symbols, so it's not pointing to a literal bottomless pit. Interestingly, Mohammed received the Qur'an while he was meditating in the Cave of Hira (an *abyss*) near Mecca in Saudi Arabia.

Mohammed proclaims that he was commanded by the archangel Gabriel to write down the words of the Qur'an, but his description of the events clearly shows that it may have been Satan or one of the fallen angels pressing on his chest.

Or perhaps it's pointing to demonic possession of Mohammed. The false religion of Islam has *darkened* the true Gospel of Messiah, the *Sun of Righteousness*.

Revelation 11:7 *"And when they shall have finished their testimony, the beast that ascendeth out of the bottomless pit shall make war against them, and shall overcome them, and kill them."*

Revelation 17:8 *"The beast that thou sawest was, and is not; and shall ascend out of the bottomless pit, and go into perdition: and they that dwell on the earth shall wonder, whose names were not written in the book of life from the foundation of the world, when they behold the beast that was, and is not, and yet is."*

Revelation 20:1,3 *"And I saw an angel come down from heaven, having the key of the bottomless pit and a great chain in his hand. And cast him into the bottomless pit, and shut him up, and set a seal upon him, that he should deceive the nations no more, till the thousand years should be fulfilled: and after that he must be loosed a little season."*

The antichrist beast doesn't literally ascend out of a bottomless pit. It's saying that Satan, who is from the *deep pit*, the *abyss*, empowers the antichrist to make war with the saints. A deep pit can exist on a flat earth or globe earth, so it's not a flat earth proof.

None of the verses cited in this section proved that the earth is flat.

"I am he that liveth, and was dead; and, behold, I am alive for evermore, Amen; and have the keys of hell and of death."
Revelation 1:18

CHAPTER 33

Everyone Sees Jesus

Nathan cites Revelation 1:7 *"Behold, he cometh with clouds; and every eye shall see him, and they also which pierced him: and all kindreds of the earth shall wail because of him. Even so, Amen."*

In his book, Nathan proposes that a giant Jesus, who is bigger and higher than the flat earth sun (which he says is 300 - 3,000 miles high), would be seen from everywhere on the flat earth. Then he asks, *"Do you fervently believe all of God's word to be faithful and true?"*

Seriously? Do you see how he has to pervert things to make verses seem like they prove that the earth is flat? If a giant Messiah returned to the center of the flat earth, not everyone could see Him, as not everyone can see the North Star.

It's simply saying that the event of Messiah *coming with clouds* is so epic, that nobody can miss it.

This verse doesn't prove a flat earth or globe earth, and his explanation of a giant Jesus is absurd!

"Let us be glad and rejoice, and give honour to him: for the marriage of the Lamb is come, and his wife hath made herself ready. And to her was granted that she should be arrayed in fine linen, clean and white: for the fine linen is the righteousness of saints. And he saith unto me, Write, Blessed are they which are called unto the marriage supper of the Lamb. And he saith unto me, These are the true sayings of God."
Revelation 19:7-9

CHAPTER 34

New Jerusalem, the HUGE cube

Nathan cites Revelation 21:15-17 *"And he that talked with me had a golden reed to measure the city, and the gates thereof, and the wall thereof. And the city lieth foursquare, and the length is as large as the breadth: and he measured the city with the reed, twelve thousand furlongs. The length and the breadth and the height of it are equal. And he measured the wall thereof, an hundred and forty and four cubits, according to the measure of a man, that is, of the angel."*

Nathan is proclaiming that due to its size, the New Jerusalem won't fit on a curved globe earth surface, but only a flat earth surface. The text isn't declaring that the bottom of the city is flat; so it doesn't need to be set on a flat surface.

That aside, is this passage pointing to an actual city, or is it an analogy which describes the vast organization of set-apart saints?

Revelation 3:12 proclaims that the overcoming saints will be made into a *pillar* in the temple of Yahuah. It's not talking about a real temple, but rather the church of Messiah. It's proclaiming that they will be a *leader* in Messiah's assembly of saints.

"Him that overcometh will I make a pillar in the temple of my God, and he shall go no more out: and I will write upon him the name of my God, and the name of the city of my God, which is new Jerusalem, which cometh down out of heaven from my God: and I will write upon him my new name."

When you read the book of Revelation, you see that the bride of Messiah is symbolically called *New Jerusalem*.

"And I John saw the holy city, new Jerusalem, coming down from God out of heaven, prepared as a bride adorned for her husband. And I heard a great voice out of heaven saying, Behold, the tabernacle of God is with men, and he will dwell with them, and they shall be his people, and God himself shall be with them, and be their God." Revelation 21:2-3

John proclaims that the bride of Messiah is the holy city, the New Jerusalem: *"Come hither, I will shew thee the bride, the Lamb's wife. And he carried me away in the spirit to a great and high mountain, and shewed me that great city, the holy Jerusalem, descending out of heaven from God."* Revelation 21:9-10

The true temple is made by His hands, *"Now, therefore, you are no longer strangers and foreigners, but fellow citizens with the saints and members of the household of God, having been built on the foundation of the apostles and prophets, Jesus Christ Himself being the chief cornerstone, in whom the whole building, being joined together, grows into a holy temple in the Lord, in whom you also are being built together for a dwelling place of God in the Spirit."* Ephesians 2:19-22

The followers of Messiah are the stones which build up the walls. *"Ye also, as lively stones, are built up a spiritual house, an holy priesthood, to offer up spiritual sacrifices, acceptable to God by Jesus Christ. Wherefore also it is contained in the scripture, Behold, I lay in Sion a chief corner stone, elect, precious: and he that believeth on him shall not be confounded. Unto you therefore which believe he is precious: but unto them which be disobedient, the stone which the builders disallowed, the same is made the head of the corner."* 1 Peter 2:4-7

We see the symbolism of New Jerusalem, so proclaiming that it's a large physical city which won't fit on a globe earth is out of context. Besides that, a city doesn't have to be flat on the bottom like Nathan is implying. His declaration that Revelation 21:15-17 are flat earth verses is built on *sinking sand.*

Interestingly, Satan is building his own city, Babylon. It has an equal width and height, and it's shaped like a pyramid. Satan is on top of the pyramid, the capstone, and his people are organized according to their levels of illumination.

Look at a Freemasonry organization chart to see an example of how this Illuminati leadership structure is setup.

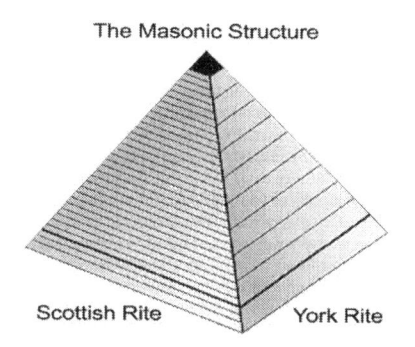

The Masonic Structure

Scottish Rite — York Rite

The people on the top levels know the Satanic agenda; while the people on the bottom levels are ordinary folks who join for business, to network and to improve themselves. This effectively hides the evil agenda of the leaders who control the Illuminati and Freemasonry, who serve Satan.

"Who, being in the form of God, thought it not robbery to be equal with God: But made himself of no reputation, and took upon him the form of a servant, and was made in the likeness of men: And being found in fashion as a man, he humbled himself, and became obedient unto death, even the death of the cross. Wherefore God also hath highly exalted him, and given him a name which is above every name: That at the name of Jesus every knee should bow, of things in heaven, and things in earth, and things under the earth."
Philippians 2:6-10

CHAPTER 35

"Breadth," spread out FLAT, of the Earth

Nathan cites Genesis 13:17, Job 38:18, Isaiah 8:8, Isaiah 42:5, ("spread out the earth"), Revelation 20:9

Genesis 13:17 *"Arise, walk through the land in the length of it and in the breadth of it; for I will give it unto thee."*

The Hebrew word for *"breadth"* is *rachab; a width:—breadth, broad place.* Yahuah is telling Abraham to walk the length and width of the *land,* which He is going to give to him and his descendants. It has nothing to do with the shape of the earth!

If I walk across the width of the modern state of Israel, does that mean that it's flat? No! This is just another example of Nathan forcing his belief that the earth is flat onto a Scripture.

Job 38:18 *"Hast thou perceived the breadth of the earth? declare if thou knowest it all."*

This verse is simply pointing to the width of the earth, which Job would not know. It doesn't prove a globe earth or a flat earth, as they both have a width. Ironically, flat-earthers don't know the width of their earth model, as they haven't measured it.

Isaiah 8:8 *"And he shall pass through Judah; he shall overflow and go over, he shall reach even to the neck; and the stretching out of his wings shall fill the breadth of thy land, O Immanuel."*

It's talking about the width of a particular area of *land*, not the whole earth; so it has nothing to do with the shape of the earth.

Isaiah 42:5 ("spread out the earth") *"Thus saith God the LORD, he that created the heavens, and stretched them out; he that spread forth the earth, and that which cometh out of it; he that giveth breath unto the people upon it, and spirit to them that walk therein:"*

Nathan is proclaiming that the words *"spread forth the earth"* are declaring that it's flat. Is all of the earth flat? No, so Nathan's eisegesis is ridiculous.

Revelation 20:9 *"And they went up on the breadth of the earth, and compassed the camp of the saints about, and the beloved city: and fire came down from God out of heaven, and devoured them."*

Pastor Dean Odle points to the word *"breadth"* and asks, *"Why didn't he just say "they went up on the earth?"* The Greek word for breadth is *platos*, which means *width*; so he looked up the etymology of the word *plateau*, which means *an elevated tract of relatively level land*. He continues with, *"So the origin of plateau which means flat land is from the Greek platys used in Revelation 20:9 to describe the earth."* Then he said that Revelation 20:9 should read, *"And they went up on the FLAT EARTH."* With this explanation, he proclaims, *"the New Testament says FLAT EARTH!"*

How is he missing that the verse says that they *went up* to the land and compassed the city, not up to the whole earth? How is he missing that the definition of *plateau* is an <u>elevated</u> tract of land, which means that all land is not elevated? I can't fathom this explanation from a pastor, who can't understand that it's talking about the elevation of the land, not the whole earth.

The Greek word for *earth* is Strong's Greek 1093 *ge*, which means: *by extension a region, or the solid part or the whole of the terrene globe (including the occupants in each application):—country, earth(-ly), ground, land, world.*

It's not referring to the whole earth, but to the *land* of Jerusalem. The armies of Gog and Magog go *up* to Jerusalem, to attack it.

Isaiah 10:32 tells us that Jerusalem is on a hill. *"As yet shall he remain at Nob that day: he shall shake his hand against the mount of the daughter of Zion, the hill of Jerusalem."*

The city of Jerusalem is at 2400 feet above the Mediterranean Sea level. Messiah and His disciples spent most of their time in places around the Sea of Galilee, which is the lowest freshwater lake on Earth, at 695 feet below the Mediterranean Sea level. Capernaum is located by the Sea of Galilee, and it sits at about 180 feet below the Mediterranean level.

So we see why they proclaimed that they were *"going up"* to Jerusalem, as it's a 2,580-foot elevation gain. Since they were in the northern area of Galilee, *"up"* cannot mean that they traveled north. It means that they walked up elevation gains on their journey to the city of Jerusalem.

"And they were in the way going up to Jerusalem; and Jesus went before them: and they were amazed; and as they followed, they were afraid. And he took again the twelve, and began to tell them what things should happen unto him." Mark 10:32

"And Joseph also went up from Galilee, out of the city of Nazareth, into Judaea, unto the city of David, which is called Bethlehem." Luke 2:4

"And when he was twelve years old, they went up to Jerusalem after the custom of the feast. They lived in Galilee, so Jerusalem was south of them, so it's not talking about going north." Luke 2:42

"And the Jews' Passover was at hand, and Jesus went up to Jerusalem," John 2:13

"After this there was a feast of the Jews; and Jesus went up to Jerusalem." John 5:1

"But when his brethren were gone up, then <u>went he also up</u> unto the feast, not openly, but as it were in secret." John 7:10

"And after those days we took up our carriages, and <u>went up to Jerusalem</u>." Acts 21:15

"Then after three years I went up to Jerusalem *to see Peter, and abode with him fifteen days."* Galatians 1:18

"Then fourteen years after I <u>went up again to Jerusalem</u> with Barnabas, and took Titus with me also." Galatians 2:1

Why did I listing so many verses? Because it reinforces the ignorance of Nathan and Pastor Dean Odle. Citing Revelation 20:9 as a flat earth verse proves nothing, except that they fail to understand the proper context of Scripture. Flat-earthers, how do you justify these verses being on the list?

"Enter ye in at the strait gate: for wide is the gate, and broad is the way, that leadeth to destruction, and many there be which go in through it: Because strait is the gate, and narrow is the way, which leadeth unto life, and few there be that find it."
Matthew 7:13-14

CHAPTER 36

Voice of Creation goes out in a "line" through all the earth

Nathan cites Psalm 19:4 *"Their line is gone out through all the earth, and their words to the end of the world. In them hath he set a tabernacle for the sun."*

Is he thinking that a line *"through all the world"* is a straight line, proving that the earth is flat? If so, that's nonsensical. The irony is that on the supposed flat earth map, the Equator line isn't straight, it goes in a circle, and the directions of east and west continually curve north.

Psalms 19:4 isn't describing a straight line, because Psalms 19:6 says that it goes in a *circuit*, so the line is a circle. *"His going forth is from the end of the heaven, and his circuit unto the ends of it: and there is nothing hid from the heat thereof."*

The *"line"* is the ecliptic *circle* of Isaiah 40:22, which surrounds the globe earth. *"It is he that sitteth upon the circle of the earth, and the inhabitants thereof are as grasshoppers; that stretcheth out the heavens as a curtain, and spreadeth them out as a tent to dwell in."*

The *"line"* is the *circuit* described in Job 22:14, *"Thick clouds are a covering to him, that he seeth not; and he walketh in the circuit of heaven."*

Psalms 19:2-4 is referring to the twelve constellations which tell the redemption story. Messiah is the *Sun of Righteousness*, who is represented by the sun, which appears in the twelve primary constellations every year.

Messiah is the *"Alpha and Omega, the beginning and the ending."* The first constellation is Virgo, which points to the virgin, Mary, the Mother of Messiah.

The last constellation is Leo, which points to Messiah *"the Lion of the tribe of Judah"* prevailing over His enemy. Indeed, Messiah is the beginning and the end of the narrative of the constellations. HalleluYah!

Do the stars on the flat earth model travel in a straight line? No, they go around in a circle, so Nathan's claim invalidates itself. Implying that a *"line"* has to be straight is *twisting* the truth.

"For the invisible things of him from the creation of the world are clearly seen, being understood by the things that are made, even his eternal power and Godhead; so that they are without excuse."
Romans 1:20

CHAPTER 37

Matthew's Bible from 1537 says "Flat Earth."

Nathan cites 2 Samuel 11:11

Matthew's Bible reads, *"And Vrias sayd vnto Dauid: the arck and Israel & Iuda dwell in pauilions: & my Lord Ioab and the seruauntes of my Lorde lye in tentes vpon the flat earthe: and shulde I then go into myne house, to eate and to dryncke & to lye wyth my wyfe? By thy lyfe and as sure as thy soule lyueth, I wyll not do that thyng."*

Nathan says, *"Now, when someone asks you, "Where does the Bible say the words 'Flat Earth?'" you are soundly equipped with a knowledgeable response."*

The King James reads, *"And Uriah said unto David, The ark, and Israel, and Judah, abide in tents; and my lord Joab, and the servants of my lord, are encamped in the <u>open fields</u>; shall I then go into mine house, to eat and to drink, and to lie with my wife? as thou livest, and as thy soul liveth, I will not do this thing."*

Nathan proclaims that *"the Bible says flat earth!"* and the 1537 Matthew's Bible does indeed use those words, but the question is, what's the context?

David had slept with Bathsheba while Uriah and his soldiers went forth to battle. When David found out that she was pregnant, he tried to get her husband Uriah to go home to sleep with her, so that it would seem that he's the father. But Uriah refused to sleep in the comfort of his home and to sleep with his wife, while his soldiers camped in the *open fields* away from their homes and wives. The context is men camping in tents in an *open field*, and it has nothing to do with the shape of the earth.

Someone commented on Nathan's Flat Earth Doctrine Facebook page about citing this as a flat earth proof, saying *"In all due fairness, the Bible in 2 Samuel says that camp was made on a flat part of the earth, not saying the whole earth was flat in that sentence or paragraphical group of thought, so not really a strong argument that helps."*

Nathan replied with, *"The reason it matters, is the Bible literal states FLAT EARTH."* By that, we can see that Nathan doesn't regard the context of the passage; he only cares that he can proclaim that the Bible says the words *"flat earth."* That's intellectual dishonesty!

The KJV Bible uses the words *"dumb ass"* in 2 Peter 2:16, but you don't see people taking it out of context. *"But was rebuked for his iniquity: the dumb ass speaking with man's voice forbad the madness of the prophet."*

Flat-earthers, every time you see Nathan proclaim that *"the Bible says flat earth,"* you now know that the context is about David, Uriah, and soldiers sleeping in tents in an *open field*. It's a shameful premise that David tried to get Uriah to sleep with his wife to try to hide his sin of adultery, and it's a shameful premise that Nathan cites this as a flat-earth verse!

"For all have sinned, and come short of the glory of God; Being justified freely by his grace through the redemption that is in Christ Jesus: Whom God hath set forth to be a propitiation through faith in his blood, to declare his righteousness for the remission of sins that are past, through the forbearance of God."
Romans 3:23-25

CHAPTER 38

Flat Earth Prophecy

Nathan cites Isaiah 40:4-5 which he says correlates with Revelation 1:7, *"Every valley shall be exalted, and every mountain and hill shall be made low: and the crooked shall be made straight, and the rough places plain: And the glory of the LORD shall be revealed, and all flesh shall see it together: for the mouth of the LORD hath spoken it."*

Isaiah 40:4-5 isn't talking about Messiah's return, but rather to His first advent. Isaiah 40:9-11 gives the context, *"O Zion, that bringest good tidings, get thee up into the high mountain; O Jerusalem, that bringest good tidings, lift up thy voice with strength; lift it up, be not afraid; say unto the cities of Judah, Behold your God! Behold, the Lord GOD will come with strong hand, and his arm shall rule for him: behold, his reward is with him, and his work before him. He shall feed his flock like a shepherd: he shall gather the lambs with his arm, and carry them in his bosom, and shall gently lead those that are with young."*

Isaiah 40:3 says, *"The voice of him that crieth in the wilderness, Prepare ye the way of the LORD, make straight in the desert a highway for our God."* It's pointing to John the Baptist, *"For this is he that was spoken of by the prophet Esaias, saying, The voice of one crying in the wilderness, Prepare ye the way of the Lord, make his paths straight."* Matthew 3:3

Nathan has repeatedly cited verses which are about John the Baptist preparing the way for Messiah, *making His way straight*; to proclaim that they're describing a flat earth. That is so very wrong! Flat-earthers, how do you justify these verses being on the list?

CHAPTER 39

Creation Worshippers
(Heliocentric Sun-god worshippers)

Nathan cites Deuteronomy 4:19, Deuteronomy 17:3, 2 Kings 23:5, Jeremiah 8:2, Acts 7:42-43, Acts 14:8-20

Deuteronomy 4:19 *"And lest thou lift up thine eyes unto heaven, and when thou seest the sun, and the moon, and the stars, even all the host of heaven, shouldest be driven to worship them, and serve them, which the LORD thy God hath divided unto all nations under the whole heaven."*

You can look up the other verses, but the focus of these nineteen verses is about pagan god worship of the sun, moon, and stars; which happens regardless of whether the earth is flat or a globe; so it doesn't prove anything. It's just another false association by Nathan to try to increase his supposed flat earth verse count. Flat-earthers, how do you justify these verses being on the list?

"Who hath delivered us from the power of darkness, and hath translated us into the kingdom of his dear Son: In whom we have redemption through his blood, even the forgiveness of sins: Who is the image of the invisible God, the firstborn of every creature: For by him were all things created, that are in heaven, and that are in earth, visible and invisible, whether they be thrones, or dominions, or principalities, or powers: all things were created by him, and for him: And he is before all things, and by him all things consist."
Colossian 1:13-17

CHAPTER 40

Lucifer/Satan's Conspiracy to unite the world against Yahuah's (God) throne which is above the Firmament

Nathan cites Genesis 11:1-9, Psalm 2, Isaiah 14:12-15, Revelation 12:7-9

Regardless of the shape of the earth, Satan is seeking to unite the world against Yahuah; so these verses don't prove that the earth is flat. The Genesis 11:1-9 story of the tower of Babel doesn't prove that the earth is flat; it simply points to man's attempt to be as god and reach the heavens.

People worshipping vain things in Psalms 2 doesn't prove the shape of the earth. Isaiah 14:12-15 is about Satan being cast down from power, which doesn't prove a flat earth.

Revelation 12:7-9 *"And there was war in heaven: Michael and his angels fought against the dragon; and the dragon fought and his angels, and prevailed not; neither was their place found any more in heaven. And the great dragon was cast out, that old serpent, called the Devil, and Satan, which deceiveth the whole world: he was cast out into the earth, and his angels were cast out with him."*

This passage is about the spiritual battle of Satan using the mighty Roman Empire to try to wipe out Messiah's assembly of saints. Recall that Satan the dragon is represented by the constellation Draco. He persecuted the saints, Messiah's *'little flock'* of sheep.

None of the twenty-eight verses in this section prove anything about the shape of the earth, so they should not be on a list of verses that supposedly proclaim that the earth is flat! Flat-earthers, how do you justify these verses being on the list?

CHAPTER 41

God's Word is ALWAYS Faithful and True

Nathan cites Jeremiah 42:5, Revelation 3:14, Revelation 19:11, Revelation 21:5, Revelation 22:6

Jeremiah 42:5 *"Then they said to Jeremiah, The LORD be a true and faithful witness between us, if we do not even according to all things for the which the LORD thy God shall send thee to us."*

HalleluYah, Yahuah is true and faithful!

Revelation 3:14 *"And unto the angel of the church of the Laodiceans write; These things saith the Amen, the faithful and true witness, the beginning of the creation of God."*

The sad irony of Nathan citing this verse is that we live in the end times generation of the church era of Laodecia, of which Messiah proclaimed: *"Because thou sayest, I am rich, and increased with goods, and have need of nothing; and knowest not that thou art wretched, and miserable, and poor, and blind, and naked: I counsel thee to buy of me gold tried in the fire, that thou mayest be rich; and white raiment, that thou mayest be clothed, and that the shame of thy nakedness do not appear; and anoint thine eyes with eyesalve, that thou mayest see. As many as I love, I rebuke and chasten: be zealous therefore, and repent."*

Flat earthers think that they're *rich*, in that they believe they have special knowledge which has been hidden from the rest of the world. But their *nakedness* has been exposed, for the verses that they cite are a *shame* on themselves.

I pray that Yahuah gives them *eyesalve*, so that the scales of the Jesuit's flat earth deceptions fall away from their eyes; so that they *may see* the truth about what Scripture is proclaiming.

Revelation 19:11 *"And I saw heaven opened, and behold a white horse; and he that sat upon him was called Faithful and True, and in righteousness he doth judge and make war."*

Revelation 21:5 *"And he that sat upon the throne said, Behold, I make all things new. And he said unto me, Write: for these words are true and faithful."*

Revelation 22:6 *"And he said unto me, These sayings are faithful and true: and the Lord God of the holy prophets sent his angel to shew unto his servants the things which must shortly be done."*

Yes, the Heavenly Father's Word is always faithful and true, but these verses do not prove that the earth is flat.

Nathan implies that if you don't believe his flat earth list, then you're denying Yahuah. The irony is that Nathan's flat earth verse explanations are not *faithful and true* to the Yahuah's Word.

That's five more verses that do not proclaim that the earth is flat. Flat-earthers, how do you justify these verses being on the list?

"And from Jesus Christ, who is the faithful witness, and the first begotten of the dead, and the prince of the kings of the earth. Unto him that loved us, and washed us from our sins in his own blood, And hath made us kings and priests unto God and his Father; to him be glory and dominion for ever and ever. Amen."
Revelation 1:5-6

CHAPTER 42
Flat Earth Verse List Conclusion

How many flat earth proof verses did you see? I don't think that I'm biased in saying that there are zero flat earth proofs on Nathan's list. The only thing that he has proven is his ignorance of the context of Scripture.

I saw that a geocentric earth could have been created before the sun, so saying *"Earth Created Before the Sun"* doesn't prove that the earth is flat.

I saw *"Earth has Pillars and hangs on nothing"* verses that point to leaders, not actual physical pillars, so they're not flat earth proofs.

I saw nonsensical statements like; *"Universe is Complete, NOT ever expanding," "Earth Measurements Unknown," "Earth Measured with a Line, not a curve," "Extremely Large Area of Land is FLAT, no curvature," "A "PLAIN" can't exist on a ball, only a "FLAT/LEVEL" surface," "Waters are Straight, not curved," "Earthquakes shake Earth, and does not move," "Earth has a Face (a geometrical flat surface)," "Waters have a Face (a geometrical flat surface)"* and *"Sky has a Face (a geometrical flat surface)."*

I saw these statements disproved; *"Moon has its own Light," "High Altitude Perspectives," "Hell is a bottomless pit at the heart of the [flat disc] earth," "Everyone Sees Jesus," "New Jerusalem, the HUGE cube," "Breadth", spread out FLAT, of the Earth,"* and *"Voice of Creation goes out in a "line" through all the earth."*

I saw no proof of *"The Firmament/Dome/Vaulted Dome, and expanse created thereby and upon where God's throne exists"* verses describing a glass dome, just the clear definition of *"And God called the firmament Heaven."* Genesis 1:8

I saw many verses which declared that *heaven was spread out*, not a glass dome.

I saw Nathan twisting Scripture to make it seem like it's pointing to a flat earth. The most blatant examples were the five verses that he cites, which are about John the Baptist *preparing the way for Messiah and making His paths straight*. Listing those as flat-earth verses is an outright abuse of Scripture!

I saw sections that have nothing to do with the shape of the earth; such as *"Be still, and know that I am God," "Creation Worshippers (Heliocentric Sun-god worshippers)," "Lucifer/Satan's Conspiracy to unite the world against Yahuah's (God) throne which is above the Firmament"* and *"God's Word is ALWAYS Faithful and True."*

I saw that Isaiah 43:5-6 tells us what the *"ends of the earth"* are, the four cardinal directions; north, east, south and west; so the many *"ends of the earth"* verses aren't flat earth proofs. *"Fear not: for I am with thee: I will bring thy seed from the east, and gather thee from the west; I will say to the north, Give up; and to the south, Keep not back: bring my sons from far, and my daughters from the ends of the earth."*

I saw that 1 Chronicles 9:24 tells us that the four quarters are the four wind directions, *"In four quarters were the porters, toward the east, west, north, and south;"* so proclaiming that the flat earth has corners (outside of the dome or at the North Pole) makes no sense.

I saw Nathan citing many verses about the *sun rising* and *going down* to proclaim that *"the sun moves,"* but the sun doesn't move up or down on the flat earth. If taken literally, then that only applies to the geocentric globe earth model. If taken symbolically, they don't prove that the earth is flat.

I saw *"Earth is fixed and immovable," "Sun Moves, not the Earth," "Sun STOPS moving,"* and *"Sun moves BACKWARDS"* verses that can be true on a geocentric globe earth, so they're not flat earth proofs.

I saw Nathan citing the 1537 Matthew's Bible, to be able to say that the *"Bible says flat earth,"* but we can see that the context of the *"flat earth"* is an *"open field"* where Uriah's men were camped in tents.

I saw the hypocrisy of Nathan citing the experiments of George Bidell Airy and Michelson-Morley to proclaim that the earth is not moving, implying that they're flat-earth proofs. Surely Nathan knows that those experiments are based on the scientific principles of a globe earth and that those scientists did not believe that the earth is flat!

Nathan Roberts is either disillusioned so badly that he can't discern the proper context of Scripture and scientific experiments, or he's deceivingly casting it aside to push his flat-earth beliefs. Either way, there's a major lack of intellectual integrity from Nathan.

Nathan has repeatedly challenged people to refute his flat earth Bible verse list. I believe that I've accomplished that goal, but I didn't just disprove his list; I showed you how some of the primary verses which flat-earthers cite, prove that the earth is a globe.

"Let us hear the conclusion of the whole matter: Fear God, and keep his commandments: for this is the whole duty of man."
Ecclesiastes 12:13

CHAPTER 43

The Cosmological Gospel Proves That The Earth Is A Globe

Nathan Roberts hands out business cards which proclaim that he's a *Cosmological Evangelist*. That's ironic as the Gospel is declared in the forty-eight constellations of the celestial sphere which surrounds the globe earth. Long before the Gospel was written down; the cosmological Gospel was written in the stars, which proclaim it night after night.

Flat-earthers can't explain how the planets appear to move through the constellations; or how planets retrograde, meaning they appear to be going backward. So they have to dismiss planets, saying that they're not real and that they're a NASA fabrication.

The description of the Flat Earth page on Facebook says, *"The Earth is still. It does not move. The surface of Earth is flat. There is a dome over us called the Firmament. The sun, moon, and stars are under the Firmament dome. The sun and moon are much smaller and closer than we are told. The sun and moon move in their own patterns over the surface of Earth.* <u>*There are no planets*</u>*. Just stars in the sky. There is no space."*

We can invalidate that claim, as we can see Mars, Venus, Mercury, Jupiter, and Saturn; if you know when and where to look. And we know that ancient cultures revered the planets and understood what they look like, such as Jupiter with its rings.

Flat-earthers ignore the witness of the many professional and amateur astrophotographers around the world, who aren't trying to prove that the earth is a globe; they just love the beauty of the heavenly bodies. They use powerful cameras and telescopes to see the planets and stars.

All you have to do to prove it for yourself is to find events from amateur astronomy clubs, to view the moon and the planets. They have no agenda, and they're not part of some conspiracy. Go see the heavenly bodies for yourself.

Flat-earthers have no explanation for how the constellations rotate above the flat earth to be in sync with the sun. In a video, Mark Sargent said, *"the stars are just lights in the sky."* The stars are very important to our Heavenly Father, *"He telleth the number of the stars; he calleth them all by their names."* Psalms 147:4

Job knew the redemption story through the stars.

Job is considered to be the oldest written book, so how did Job understand that a Redeemer would come? Job 19:25-27 says, *"For I know that my redeemer liveth, and that he shall stand at the latter day upon the earth: And though after my skin worms destroy this body, yet in my flesh shall I see God: Whom I shall see for myself, and mine eyes shall behold, and not another; though my reins be consumed within me."*

Five constellations are referred to by name in the book of Job: *Arcturus, Orion, and Pleiades* in Job 9:9; *Pleiades, Orion and the Bear with her sons* in Job 38:31-33; *the crooked serpent* (Hydra) in Job 26:13; and the whole zodiac circle of constellations, the *Mazzaroth*, with its succession of signs and seasons, is spoken of in Job 38:32.

At an early age of human existence, our Creator led His set-apart people in understanding the names and groupings of the stars; to show them the Gospel message which is proclaimed in the expanse of the heavens. They've been in the star-charts of cultures for thousands of years.

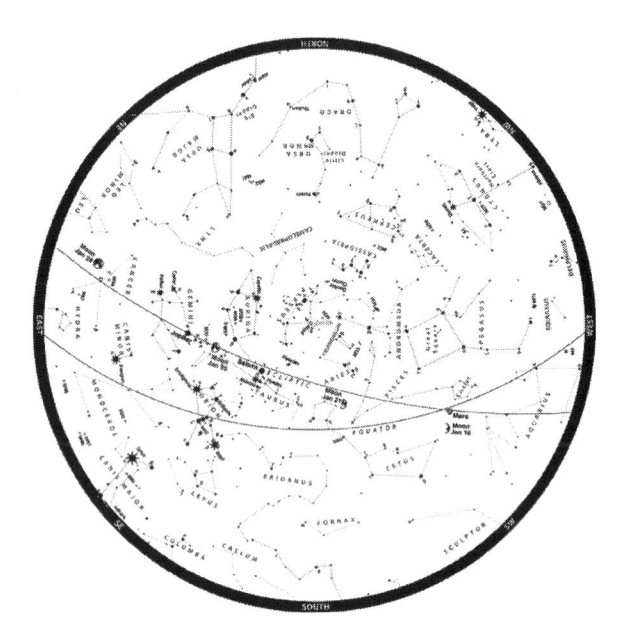

Here's a summary of the redemption story that's told in the stars.

E.W. Bullinger, in his book *The Witness of the Stars*, said: *"These pictures were designed to preserve, expound, and perpetuate the one first great promise, that all hope for Man, all hope for Creation, was bound up in a coming Redeemer; One who should be born of a woman; who should first suffer, and afterwards gloriously triumph; One who should first be wounded by that great enemy who was the cause of all sin and sorrow and death, but who should finally crush the head of "that Old Serpent the Devil."*

Ken Fleming, in his book *God's Voice in the Stars*, said: *"In the first four signs Christ is portrayed as the Suffering Savior delivering man from the penalty of sin. In the middle four signs Christ is portrayed as the Glorified Blesser delivering man from the power of sin. In the remaining four signs Christ is portrayed as the Reigning Judge delivering man from the presence of sin."*

The sign Virgo represents the Promised Seed of the woman, Messiah the incarnate Son.

The three decan constellations of Virgo are **Coma**, which points to a woman with her child, and that He should be the *"Desire of all nations."* **Centaurus**, which has two natures, holding a spear piercing a victim, Messiah the despised sin offering. And **Bootes**, which points to a man walking bearing a branch called Arcturus, meaning *"He cometh."*

"Therefore the Lord himself shall give you a sign; Behold, a virgin shall conceive, and bear a son, and shall call his name Immanuel." Isaiah 7:14

The decan constellation *Coma* represents a woman with a child on her lap, pointing to Mary, the mother of Messiah. This has been perverted by the enemy to point to the pagan goddesses of Semiramis of Babylon, Isis of Egypt, etc.

The enemy hid this truth by causing astronomers to rename *Coma* with the name *'Berenices Hair,'* after Berenice II of Egypt who sacrificed her long hair as a votive offering.

The sign Libra represents the justice and judgment of our sins, paid with a price by the blood of Messiah our Redeemer.

The three decan constellations of Libra are **Crux**, which represents the mark of the Hebrew Tav symbol, the cross of Messiah endured. **Lupus**, which represents the victim slain, Messiah's sacrifice for our sin. And **Corona**, which represents the crown which is bestowed upon our Messiah.

"Just as the Son of Man did not come to be served, but to serve, and to give His life a ransom for many." Matthew 20:28

The sign Scorpio represents the enemy seeking to wound Messiah, but itself trodden underfoot.

The three decan constellations of Scorpio are **Serpens**, which means the serpent struggling with the man, Messiah. **Ophiuchus**, which means the struggle with the enemy. And **Hercules**, which points to a man kneeling on one knee, humbled in the conflict, but victorious, our mighty Messiah.

"Thou shalt tread upon the lion and adder: the young lion and the dragon shalt thou trample under feet." Psalms 91:13

The sign Sagittarius represents the archer, going forth to conquer.

The three decans of Sagittarius are **Lyra**, which represents the praise for the victorious conqueror, Messiah. **Ara**, which represents the consuming fire prepared for His enemies. And **Draco**, which represents the old serpent cast down in defeat.

"And in thy majesty ride prosperously because of truth and meekness and righteousness; and thy right hand shall teach thee terrible things. Thine arrows are sharp in the heart of the king's enemies; whereby the people fall under thee." Psalms 45:4-5

The sign Capricorn represents the goat, the sacrificial death for the redeemed.

The three decan constellations of Capricorn are **Sagitta**, which means the arrow of Yahuah sent forth for judgment. **Aquila**, which represents the smitten One falling. And **Delphinus**, which represents the dead One, Messiah, rising again.

"Verily, verily, I say unto you, Except a corn of wheat fall into the ground and die, it abideth alone: but if it die, it bringeth forth much fruit." John 12:24

The sign Aquarius represents the living waters of blessing poured forth for the redeemed.

The three decan constellations of Aquarius are **Piscis Australis**, which represents the southern fish, the blessings bestowed. **Pegasus**, which represents the winged horse, the blessings quickly coming. And **Cygnus**, which represents the sure return of our Redeemer.

"In the last day, that great day of the feast, Jesus stood and cried, saying, If any man thirst, let him come unto me, and drink. He that believeth on me, as the scripture hath said, out of his belly shall flow rivers of living water." John 7:37-38

The sign Pisces represents the redeemed blessed by our Liberator.

The three decan constellations of Pisces are **The Band**, which represents the redeemed as bound. **Andromeda**, which represents the redeemed in their bondage and affliction. And **Cepheus**, which represents the King, the Redeemer, coming to rule.

"And he saith unto them, Follow me, and I will make you fishers of men." Matthew 4:19

The sign Aries represents the lamb that was slain, prepared for the victory.

The three decan constellations of Aries are **Cassiopeia**, which represents the captive delivered, preparing for her husband, the Redeemer. **Cetus**, which represents the sea monster, the great enemy bound. And **Perseus**, which represents the breaker, Messiah, delivering His redeemed.

"Saying with a loud voice, Worthy is the Lamb that was slain to receive power, and riches, and wisdom, and strength, and honor, and glory, and blessing." Revelation 5:12

The sign Taurus represents Messiah the wild bull coming to rule.

The three decan constellations of Taurus are **Orion**, which represents the light breaking forth in the person of the Redeemer. **Eridanus**, which represents the fiery wrath breaking forth on His enemies. And **Auriga**, which represents the protection of His people in the day of that wrath.

Messiah declared that he's the *Alpha and the Omega*, which are the first and last letters of the Greek alphabet. In the Hebrew alphabet, they are the *Aleph and the Tav*. The symbol for the Aleph is an ox head, and it means *strength* and *leader*.

"I am Alpha and Omega, the beginning and the end, the first and the last." Revelation 22:13

The sign Gemini represents the two-fold nature of the King.

The three decan constellations of Gemini are **Lepus**, which represents the enemy trodden underfoot. **Major Sirius**, which represents the coming glorious Prince. And **Canis Minor**, which represents the exalted Redeemer.

"Looking unto Jesus, the author and finisher of our faith, who for the joy that was set before Him endured the cross, despising the shame, and has sat down at the right hand of the throne of God." Hebrews 12:2

The sign Cancer represents the possession, the redeemed, held secure by Messiah.

The three decan constellations of Cancer are **Ursa Minor**, which represents the lesser sheepfold. **Ursa Major**, which represents the fold and the flock. And **Argo**, which represents the redeemed pilgrims safe at home.

"While I was with them in the world, I kept them in thy name: those that thou gavest me I have kept, and none of them is lost, but the son of perdition; that the scripture might be fulfilled." John 17:12

The sign Leo represents the Lion of the Tribe of Judah aroused for the rending of the enemy.

The three decan constellations of Leo are **Hydra**, which represents that old serpent, the devil, destroyed. **Crater**, which represents the cup of divine wrath poured out on the serpent. And **Corvus**, which represents the birds of prey devouring the old serpent.

"And one of the elders saith unto me, Weep not: behold, the Lion of the tribe of Judah, the Root of David, hath prevailed to open the book, and to loose the seven seals thereof." Revelation 5:5

Messiah is the *Alpha and Omega* not only in Scripture from Genesis to Revelation, but also from Virgo to Leo in the Celestial Gospel of the mazzaroth. Even the Great Sphinx in Egypt points to this ancient message in the stars, as it unifies the first and last signs of the Biblical mazzaroth in the head of the woman Virgo with the body of the Lion Leo.

The word Sphinx means *'to bind together.'* It was therefore designed to show where the two ends of the Zodiac are joined together, where the great circle of the heavens begins and ends.

When flat-earthers dismiss the importance of the stars, they're inadvertently dismissing the Gospel narrative which is proclaimed in the tabernacle of stars that make up the celestial sphere. They're dismissing the symbolism of Psalms 19:1-6, in which the *Sun of Righteousness*, Messiah, is running the race to redeem His set apart saints; as the Gospel is proclaimed every year when the sun appears in the twelve constellations of the ecliptic circle.

Here are some additional Bible verses that proclaim the importance of the stars.

"Seek him that maketh the seven stars and Orion, and turneth the shadow of death into the morning, and maketh the day dark with night: that calleth for the waters of the sea, and poureth them out upon the face of the earth: The LORD is his name." Amos 5:8

Matthew 2:2, 9-10 is pointing to the star of Bethlehem, *"Saying, Where is he that is born King of the Jews? for we have seen his star in the east, and are come to worship him. When they had heard the king, they departed; and, lo, the star, which they saw in the east, went before them, till it came and stood over where the young child was. When they saw the star, they rejoiced with exceeding great joy."*

"I have made the earth, and created man upon it: I, even my hands, have stretched out the heavens, and all their host have I commanded." Isaiah 45:12

Venus is the *"morning star"* and it can be seen twenty minutes before sunrise. It's one of the most beautiful objects in the sky. When we see it, we ought to think of our Messiah; whose love, grace and mercy, is new every morning.

Flat-earthers dismiss the planets and constellations because they have no way to explain how they work on the flat earth model. But you can go to local astronomy club events to see them for yourself.

We live in a technologically advanced age, where we have access to more information than those who have gone before us.

Stellarium is a free open source planetarium for your computer, showing you where to look for planets and constellations. It shows a realistic sky in 3D, just like what you see with the naked eye, binoculars, or a telescope.

The SkyView App brings stargazing to everyone, as you point your phone or tablet at the sky to identify stars, constellations, satellites, etc. It lets you track the constellations and planets in real-time so that you can see where they are in the sky. You can track the moon on the opposite side of the earth, to watch it move towards the eastern horizon and appear in your sky.

TheSkyLive.com provides accurate real-time data and finder charts for the most interesting Solar System objects. Those and many other resources are available to us, and they all prove the forty-eight constellations that make up the whole celestial sphere, which surrounds the globe earth.

How in the world do people believe that the earth is flat with a dome over it when they have access to all of this information?

It's a huge leap of faith to proclaim that all of those programs are manipulating the information that's really on the flat earth, to make it seem like it's a globe earth.

Flat-earthers have to dismiss a lot of things to try to justify the flat earth model, which have scientific explanations on the globe earth model. The truth is that flat-earthers have no scientific explanations, just CGI. The flat earth is false science, which steals glory away from the Creator.

1 Timothy 6:20 says, *"O Timothy, keep that which is committed to thy trust, avoiding profane and vain babblings, and oppositions of science falsely so called."*

"And as Moses lifted up the serpent in the wilderness, even so must the Son of man be lifted up: That whosoever believeth in him should not perish, but have eternal life. For God so loved the world, that he gave his only begotten Son, that whosoever believeth in him should not perish, but have everlasting life.

For God sent not his Son into the world to condemn the world; but that the world through him might be saved. He that believeth on him is not condemned: but he that believeth not is condemned already, because he hath not believed in the name of the only begotten Son of God.

And this is the condemnation, that light is come into the world, and men loved darkness rather than light, because their deeds were evil. For every one that doeth evil hateth the light, neither cometh to the light, lest his deeds should be reproved. But he that doeth truth cometh to the light, that his deeds may be made manifest, that they are wrought in God"
John 3:14-21

CHAPTER 44
Globe Earth Verses

My initial purpose in writing this book was only to expose how flat-earthers are taking verses out of context, but as I studied the context of the verses, I saw that some of them describe a globe earth. I've given detailed explanations about these verses in previous chapters, but I'm going to summarize them here so that you can see their collective witness, and I've added some information.

Proverbs 8:27 *"When he prepared the heavens, I was there: when he set a compass upon the face of the depth."*

This is explained in detail in the *Earth is a Disk/Circle, not a ball* chapter. Flat-earthers say that the *"compass"* is the circular ice wall that surrounds the vast oceans; but the text says that the compass, the circle, is *upon* the face of the depth, not *around* it. The next verse points to the *fountains of the deep*. It's not pointing to the oceans being held in place by an ice wall; rather, it's pointing to the water which is stored under the upper layers of the globe earth.

Genesis 1:2 describes an earth that was covered by water, and then some of the water was commanded under the earth to reveal the land. Genesis 1:9-10, Job 26:10, Psalms 24:1-2, Proverbs 8:28-29 and Psalms 104:5-9; all describe the deep fountains which are bound under the *circular* layers of the earth.

The flood narrative describes this water being released to cover the land, and then it was commanded to retreat under the earth. Geologists believe that a layer of a mineral called *ringwoodite*, which is found 400 miles beneath the Earth's surface, may hold three times the amount of water found in Earth's oceans.

We can see how Scripture is pointing to these deep waters which are *compassed*, and we can see how that occurs on the circular layers of the globe earth.

Isaiah 40:22 *"It is he that sitteth upon the circle of the earth, and the inhabitants thereof are as grasshoppers; that stretcheth out the heavens as a curtain, and spreadeth them out as a tent to dwell in."*

This is explained in detail in the *Earth is a Disk/Circle, not a ball* chapter. Isaiah knows the difference between a *ball* and a *circle*, so if Isaiah is describing the globe earth, then he would have used the word *ball* (Strong's Hebrew 1754, *duwr*), not *circle* (Strong's Hebrew 2329, *chuwg*).

If Isaiah is describing a flat disc earth, then he could have used the Hebrew word *round* (5696 `agol*). 1 Kings 7:23, 1 Kings 7:35 and 2 Chronicles 4:2; use the word *round* to describe a disc-shaped object, so it's a more accurate word to describe a disc flat earth. But Isaiah didn't use the word *"round"* to describe a disc-shaped earth, and he didn't use the word *"ball"* to describe a globe-shaped earth; as he's not describing the earth itself.

Isaiah 40:22 doesn't say *"circle earth,"* it says *"the circle of the earth."* The *circle* is the focus. Just as you would say *"the ring of Saturn"* to point to the ring, not the planet; Isaiah is pointing to the *ecliptic circle* which surrounds the globe earth and declares the Gospel story in the twelve constellations.

Isaiah 40:22 says, *"It is he that sitteth upon the circle of the earth."* The *'he'* is our Heavenly Father, who is not sitting on the earth, so we can see that the *circle* is not describing the earth. It says *"and the inhabitants thereof are as grasshoppers"* which reveals that Yahuah's viewpoint makes people look small, as He is high above, once again proving that He's not sitting on a circle earth.

The same Hebrew word (*chuwg*) is used in Job 22:14 to describe the *circuit of heaven*, which also proves that Yahuah walks on the *circle of heaven*, not on the earth. *"Thick clouds are a covering to him, that he seeth not; and he walketh in the circuit of heaven."*

In the context of talking about the *circle*, Isaiah describes the stars, not the earth; *"that stretcheth out the heavens as a curtain, and spreadeth them out as a tent to dwell in."*

Look at the image on the cover of the book. Yahuah's home is in the *tabernacle* of stars which surrounds the globe earth as a *curtain*.

The twelve constellations on the ecliptic *circle* have proclaimed His Gospel plan of redemption from the beginning. The thirty-six decan constellations surround the earth as a *tent*, from the north celestial pole to the south celestial pole.

Isaiah 40:21 points to the stars, *"Did you not know? Have you not heard? Has it not been declared to you from the beginning? Have you not understood from the foundations of the earth?"*

In Isaiah 40:26, Yahuah tells Isaiah to look up to the *circle* of the stars (*host*) of the mazzaroth. *"Lift up your eyes on high and see. Who has created these? He who is bringing out their host by number, He calls them all by name, by the greatness of His might and the strength of His power – not one is missing."*

The non-canonical Book of Wisdom (aka Wisdom of Solomon), which was written in the 1st century B.C., points to the circle of stars, *"But deemed either fire, or wind, or the swift air, or <u>the circle of the stars</u>, or the violent water, or the lights of heaven, to be the gods which govern the world."* Wisdom of Solomon 13:2

2 Enoch 21:7-8 points to the twelve constellations of the circle of the expanse of heaven, *"And I saw the eighth heaven, which is called in the Hebrew tongue Muzaloth, changer of the seasons, of drought, and of wet, and of <u>the twelve constellations of the circle of the firmament,</u> which are above the seventh heaven. And I saw the ninth heaven, which is called in Hebrew Kuchavim, where are the heavenly homes of the twelve constellations of the circle of the firmament."*

Satan caused different cultures to pervert the stories of the constellations, making them about pagan gods, to hide that they surround the globe earth to proclaim the Gospel.

Isaiah 40:21-26 is describing the ecliptic *circle* in which the twelve constellations reside, and ultimately to the thirty-six decan constellations which form a global celestial sphere that surrounds the globe earth as a *tent*, as a *tabernacle* in which Yahuah dwells.

Job 26:7 *"He stretcheth out the north over the empty place, and hangeth the earth upon nothing."*

This is explained in detail in the *Firmament/Dome/Vaulted Dome* chapter. What's being *stretched*? Job 9:8, Psalms 104:2, Isaiah 42:5, Isaiah 44:24, Isaiah 45:12, Isaiah 48:13, Isaiah 51:13, Jeremiah 10:12, Jeremiah 51:15 and Zechariah 12:1; all declare that it's the *heavens which are stretched out*.

What Job 26:7 is proclaiming is *"stretched out"* is the heavenly celestial sphere, which rotates below the North Star. Look at the cover of this book. In the middle of the canopy of stars is a vast space, in which the jewel of the universe, the earth, is *hung upon nothing*. There are programs such as Stellarium which let you see the whole celestial sphere which surrounds the globe earth.

Job 26:7 is a proof of the globe earth and the planisphere of constellations around it; the *firmament* of *expanse* of *heaven*, the *curtain* of stars, the *tabernacle* of Yahuah.

Job 38:13-14 *"That it might take hold of the ends of the earth, that the wicked might be shaken out of it? It is turned as clay to the seal, and they stand as a garment."*

This is explained in detail in the *Earth is a Disk/Circle, not a ball* chapter. Flat-earthers proclaim that the earth was like a flat surface of clay on which Yahuah used a stamp to form the shape. It does not say *"It was turned as clay to the seal"* to point back to a creation event, it says *"It is turned as clay to the seal"* to point to the continuous action of the sun.

We can see that it's not about a creation event, as it points to wicked men who existed at the time. Read Job 38:12-20, and you notice that the context is about *light*. The verses include the words; *morning, dayspring, light is withheld, shadow, where light dwelleth,* and *darkness;* and it mentions *"wicked men"* twice.

The context is the light hitting the earth, as Job 38:12 is talking about the morning and dawn knowing its place. *"Hast thou commanded the morning since thy days, and caused the dayspring to know his place."*

It's declaring that the Earth is changed, it's transformed, as the sun removes the darkness. It's proclaiming that as the sun rises and brings light on the earth, that the deeds of the wicked are exposed so that their power and strength is broken.

The patterns of the sun on the globe earth change during the year, causing the sun to rise at different positions, changing the length of daylight, and creating the different seasons; thus the *dayspring knows its place*, as it follows the Creator's commands.

Job 38:19-20 is talking about darkness knowing its place, its boundary. *"Where is the way where light dwelleth? and as for darkness, where is the place thereof, That thou shouldest take it to the bound thereof, and that thou shouldest know the paths to the house thereof?"*

How does darkness know its place, its boundary? The curve of the earth limits where the sun shines; it creates this clear delineation.

It's pointing to the physical properties of the globe earth, which separate the light from the dark. The rays of the sun are parted, separated so that they don't shine on the other side of the globe.

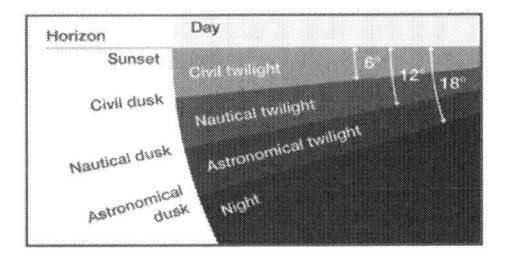

We see the predictable transition of the darkness to light in the morning, and light to darkness in the evening. When the sun is 18 degrees below the horizon, it's completely dark.

There's nothing on the flat earth model to create this boundary, no definite thing that stops the sun from shining on certain parts of the world, no delineation where darkness rules the night.

Job 38 is proclaiming that the *wicked* like the *darkness*, but as the sun's light is turned upon them, it exposes them. The globe earth, which seemed in the night to have no form, is revealed anew when the sun rises and all things are clad with new beauty.

The context of Job 38:19-20 is about how light and darkness is delineated on the earth, which proves that the earth is a globe.

Amos 9:6 *"It is he that buildeth his stories in the heaven, and hath founded his troop in the earth; he that calleth for the waters of the sea, and poureth them out upon the face of the earth: The LORD is his name."*

The Strong's Hebrew word for *"stories"* is pointing to the *"elevation"* of heaven, the progression of spherical layers; once again pointing to how the *expanse of heaven*, the firmament, is *stretched out*.

The Septuagint, the Greek Old Testament, reads, *"It is he that builds up to the sky."* The 1568 Bishops Bible reads, *"He buildeth his spheres in the heaven."* The 1587 Geneva Bible reads, *"He buildeth his spheres in the heaven."*

This image shows the *"the spheres,"* the *stories*, which surround the globe earth; with each sphere serving a different purpose.

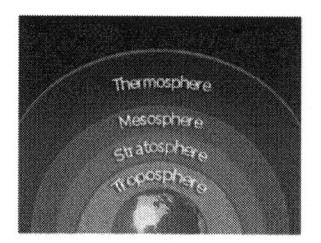

Flat-earthers proclaim that there aren't any verses which say that the earth is a globe, but we can see how Scripture describes: the fountains of the deep which are *encircled* by the layers of the globe earth; the ecliptic line that *encircles* the globe earth; the celestial *sphere* of stars which surrounds the globe earth; and the *circular* atmosphere that surrounds the globe earth in spherical layers.

This book has shown how there a *zero* Scriptural flat-earth proofs and *many* proofs of the globe earth.

CHAPTER 45
Geocentric Universe Verses

During my research for this book, it became apparent that the only model that doesn't require excuses is the geocentric globe earth model. Many verses declare that the sun rises and sets, and there's no reason not to take them literally; and that only happens on the geocentric globe earth model.

Scripture declares that the sun is *moving* and that it's been *stopped* and *moved back* under special circumstances. We've proven that Scripture is not describing a flat earth, so the only model on which the sun moves, and can be stopped and moved back, is the geocentric globe earth model. One has to make excuses to justify the heliocentric globe earth model, as the sun does not move, so it can't be *stopped* or *moved back*.

Scripture never declares that the earth rotates around the sun or that the earth is moving. Scripture only says that the earth is moved during prophetic circumstances, which point to something that's outside of the norm, such as an event in the end times.

If one is honest, without pressing their beliefs onto Scripture, there's no way to conclude that the earth is orbiting the sun. If you have to make excuses to justify your view, then you're not allowing the text to speak. Scripture should be taken literally unless the context proves otherwise.

Biblical creationists have done an amazing job at proving how the creation of the earth matches up with the Genesis account, to counter the scientific community about the age of the earth, to dismiss the theory of evolution. They demand that science be subjugated to the Bible.

Unfortunately, they've subjugated the Bible to modern science regarding the orientation of the earth in the universe. There simply is no Scriptural justification for the heliocentric model, so why do people believe it?

I say *'modern science'* because up until the 16th century, scientists and theologians believed in the geocentric model. All of that has been swept under the rug and hidden by the enemy. I pray that you can put aside your preconceived notions and take an honest look at how Scripture describes a geocentric globe earth model.

Genesis creation

On the first day of creation, there was no heaven and no sun, just the earth. If you were building a universe, would you not start with the center and build around it?

On the second day, Yahuah created the expanse of heaven, the sphere of the sky which surrounds the earth. It's declaring that the heavens encircle the earth, not the sun.

On the third day, the water on the earth was separated, some placed above the earthly heavens, and some placed below the earth's mantle, so that dry land appeared.

On the fourth day, the sun and moon were created to give *light*, to *rule*, and to *divide*. Their functions are *"for signs" "for seasons" "for days"* and *"for years."* Scripture declares that the sun and moon are in the earth-centered expanse of heaven. It makes sense that both of those lights are moving to declare these signs to those who are on the earth.

Does Scripture say that the earth was put in motion around the sun? No. Does it make any sense to create the earth first, then create the sun, and then start the earth rotating around the sun? No.

The creation account of *the heaven and the earth* through the first four days describes an earth-centered universe.

A literal and contextual interpretation of Genesis 1:1-19 proves that our Creator designed a geocentric earth that's surrounded by the three heavens: the lower expanse in which the birds fly, and clouds exist; the middle expanse in which the stars and planets exist; and the top expanse where our Creator resides.

If you insist that the creation narrative points to a heliocentric earth, what in the Bible justifies that position? If you know of any verses, please share them on the book feedback page.

Job proclaims that the heavens have a circuit.

"Thick clouds are a covering to him, that he seeth not; and he walketh in the circuit of heaven." Job 22:14

Scripture declares that the heavens surround the earth, not the sun; so the *circuit of heaven* in Job 22:14 is earth-centered. Scripture declares that the heavens have a circuit and that the sun has a circuit (Psalms 19:4-6), but nowhere does the Bible say that the earth follows a circular path.

In Psalms 19:1-6, David describes the sun running its path, and traveling in a circuit.

"The heavens are proclaiming the esteem of Ĕl; And the expanse is declaring the work of His hand. Day to day pours forth speech, And night to night reveals knowledge. There is no speech, and there are no words, Their voice is not heard. Their line has gone out through all the earth, And their words to the end of the world. In them He set up a tent for the sun, And it is like a bridegroom coming out of his room, It rejoices like a strong man to run the path. Its rising is from one end of the heavens, And its circuit to the other end; And naught is hidden from its heat."

The verbs about the sun describe its movement: *"comes out," "to run," "his race,"* and *"goes forth"* through its complete *"circuit."* One has to make excuses to say that Psalms 19:1-6 does not mean that the sun is running its path in the circuit of heaven.

Yahuah's throne is above the earth.

Joshua 2:11 proclaims that the earth is below the heaven where Yahuah resides, *"And as soon as we had heard these things, our hearts did melt, neither did there remain any more courage in any man, because of you: for the LORD your God, he is God in heaven above, and in earth beneath."*

Isaiah 66:1 says that the earth is the footstool under the throne of Yahuah, *"Thus saith the LORD, The heaven is my throne, and the earth is my footstool: where is the house that ye build unto me? and where is the place of my rest?"*

Psalms 102:19 says the Yahuah looks from His sanctuary, down to the earth, *"For he hath looked down from the height of his sanctuary; from heaven did the LORD behold the earth;"*

Psalms 103:11 says that the heaven of Yahuah is above the earth, *"For as the heaven is high above the earth, so great is his mercy toward them that fear him."*

On the heliocentric model, the earth reportedly flies through space at 66,600 MPH as it orbits the sun. The sun and all the planets in the solar system are spinning around the center of the Milky Way, while at the same time moving upwards relative to the Milky Way plane, which means that we're reportedly moving through the galaxy at approximately 541,700 MPH. And that's not even counting the fact that our Milky Way is also zooming through the universe.

Do we imagine that Yahuah's throne is also flying through space to stay above the earth? Doesn't it make more sense that the earth is still in the universe and not speeding through space and that our Heavenly Father's throne resides above it?

A geocentric, non-moving earth is a more logical fit, and you'll see in an upcoming chapter that scientific experiments which were designed to prove that the earth is moving, actually proved the very opposite.

These verses make declarations from the sun's perspective

People dismiss verses by saying that they're talking about our perspective, that it only seems like the sun is moving; but these verses are from the sun's perspective, so we can't dismiss the literal explanation.

"So let all thine enemies perish, O LORD: but let them that love him be as the sun when he goeth forth in his might. And the land had rest forty years." Judges 5:31

"In them hath he set a tabernacle for the sun, which is as a bridegroom coming out of his chamber, and rejoiceth as a strong man to run a race. His going forth is from the end of the heaven, and his circuit unto the ends of it: and there is nothing hid from the heat thereof." Psalms 19:4-6

"He appointed the moon for seasons: the sun knoweth his going down." Psalms 104:19. The sun is following its Creator's command to move around the earth, to cause the night to come at precise times.

"The sun also ariseth, and the sun goeth down, and hasteth to his place where he arose." Ecclesiastes1:5. The word *hasteth* implies action, to travel around the earth and return to the place where it *arose* the previous day.

There's no reason to believe that Ecclesiastes 1:5 is speaking symbolically, as the passages around it are literal. Ecclesiastes 1:7, describes the water cycle of evaporation and precipitation. *"All the rivers run into the sea; yet the sea is not full; unto the place from whence the rivers come, thither they return again."*

Scriptures declare that the sun was moved back.

The context of 2 Kings 20 is that King Hezekiah was sick and near death, but because of his repentance, a sign was given that his life would be extended. The sign is that the sun would be moved back to cause its shadow to return by ten degrees. 2 Kings 20:8-9 and 2 Chronicles 32:24-26 also record this event.

Isaiah 38:8 points to this same timeframe and it says that it was the sun that was moved back ten degrees: *"Behold, I will bring again the shadow of the degrees, which is gone down in the sun dial of Ahaz, ten degrees backward. So the sun returned ten degrees, by which degrees it was gone down."* Isaiah 38:4-8

Ecclesiasticus 48:23 confirms that it was the sun which was moved, *"In his time the sun went backward, and he lengthened the king's life."*

The sun being moved backward doesn't fit with the heliocentric globe earth model. This can only be explained on the geocentric globe earth model, on which the sun can be moved backward to cause the shadow to go back ten degrees.

Scriptures declare that the sun stopped moving.

Joshua 10:12-14 *"Then spake Joshua to the LORD in the day when the LORD delivered up the Amorites before the children of Israel, and he said in the sight of Israel, Sun, stand thou still upon Gibeon; and thou, Moon, in the valley of Ajalon. <u>And the sun stood still, and the moon stayed, until the people had avenged themselves upon their enemies</u>. Is not this written in the book of Jasher?*

So the sun stood still in the midst of heaven, and hasted not to go down about a whole day. And there was no day like that before it or after it, that the LORD hearkened unto the voice of a man: for the LORD fought for Israel."

Joshua references the book of Jasher, which says, *"And when they were smiting, the day was declining toward evening, and Joshua said in the sight of all the people, <u>Sun, stand thou still upon Gibeon, and thou moon in the valley of Ajalon, until the nation shall have revenged itself upon its enemies</u>. And the Lord hearkened to the voice of Joshua, <u>and the sun stood still in the midst of the heavens</u>, and it stood still six and thirty moments, <u>and the moon also stood still and hastened not to go down a whole day</u>. <u>And there was no day like that, before it or after it</u>, that the Lord hearkened to the voice of a man, for the Lord fought for Israel."* Jasher 88:63-65

By proclaiming that the sun stood still, this tells us that it was an unusual occurrence; as the sun normally was not standing still. It declares that both the sun and moon were commanded to stay still. We know the moon rotates around the earth, so it's implying that the sun also rotates around the earth. To say that one body normally moves and the other one doesn't, when both of them are commanded not to move is bad hermeneutics.

It declares that on no other day, before or after it, has the sun stood still like this. How can we not take Scripture at its literal word?

Habakkuk 3:11 *"The sun and moon stood still in their habitation: at the light of thine arrows they went, and at the shining of thy glittering spear."*

This verse reinforces that this was a special occasion when the sun and moon were commanded not to move, confirming that they're normally in motion. People who defend the heliocentric model have to make excuses, but it fits perfectly with the geocentric globe earth model.

Scripture declares catastrophic circumstances in which the earth will be moved, which is contrary to the norm.

Job 9:6 points to earth's *"place."* A revolving earth doesn't have a set place. *"Which shaketh the earth out of her place, and the pillars thereof tremble."*

The Hebrew word for *"out of her place"* is 4725 *maqowm*; which means *properly, a standing, i.e. a spot; but used widely of a locality (general or specific); also (figuratively) of a condition (of body or mind):—country, home, open, place, room, space, whither(-soever).*

It's pointing to a *locality*, a *home*, which is not pointing to a continuous circuit. If Job was describing the earth traveling in a circuit, he could have used the word *chuwg*; which means *a circle, circuit, compass*; to say that the earth was moved out of its circuit.

Ecclesiastes 1:5-7 describes three things which move continually relative to the earth: the sun, the wind, and the rivers.

"The sun also ariseth, and the sun goeth down, and hasteth to his place where he arose. The wind goeth toward the south, and turneth about unto the north; it whirleth about continually, and the wind returneth again according to his circuits. All the rivers run into the sea; yet the sea is not full; unto the place from whence the rivers come, thither they return again."

If the sun isn't moving, then that doesn't match the description of the wind and rivers, which are moving. Instead, it's easy to see that the passage is declaring that the sun, wind, and rivers, are all moving. The sun rises on the eastern horizon, it runs its course across the sky during the day, it continues its circuit on the other side of the earth to allow nighttime, and it returns on the eastern horizon the next morning.

The verbs about the sun declare action, movement: *"riseth," "goeth down," "hasteneth,"* and *"arose."* The verbs about the wind declare movement: *"goeth," "turneth about,"* and *"returneth."* The waters have a continual flow upon the earth.

To justify the heliocentric view, one must declare that the sun only looks like it's moving from our perspective; while the wind and rain literally move. Giving a selective argument, that only the wind and water move relative to the earth, but that the sun does not, is faulty hermeneutics.

If taken literally, then all of the verses which proclaim that the sun rises and sets prove the geocentric globe earth.

This is explained in detail in the *Sun Moves, not the Earth* section. If those verses are speaking about our viewpoint, that the sun appears to rise and go down, then that fits both the heliocentric and geocentric globe earth.

But why would we not take those verses literally? Because men taught us differently? The literal explanation is congruent with the other verses which are cited in this chapter.

When taken literally, those verses don't fit with the heliocentric globe earth model, as the sun is not moving. The only model in which the sun is moving, and it literally rises and sets; is the geocentric globe earth model.

Messiah pointed to making the sun rise and to sending rain.

"That ye may be the children of your Father which is in heaven: for he maketh his sun to rise on the evil and on the good, and sendeth rain on the just and on the unjust." Matthew 5:45

One has to make excuses to say that one part of the verse is just talking about our perspective, and the other part is literal.

The verbs *"to rise"* and *"sendeth"* are describing the action of the sun and rain, respectively. There is no conflict with the geocentric model.

Here's some over verses from the Apocrypha which describe a sun that's moving.

Just because these books aren't included in the official canon of books, doesn't mean that they don't have value.

1 Esdras 4:34 points to the course of the sun, which circles the heavens, *"O ye men, are not women strong? great is the earth, high is the heaven, <u>swift is the sun in his course</u>, for he compasseth the heavens round about, and fetcheth his course again to his own place in one day."*

Psalms of Solomon 18:11-14 points to the path of the sun, *"Great is our God and glorious, dwelling in the highest. (It is He) <u>who hath established in (their) courses the lights (of heaven) for determining seasons from year to year</u>, And they have not turned aside from the way which He appointed them In the fear of God (they pursue) their path every day, From the day God created them and for evermore. And they have erred not since the day He created them. Since the generations of old they have not withdrawn from their path, Unless God commanded them (so to do) by the command of His servants."*

Jasher 68:15 points to the circuit of the sun, *"And God sent forth at that time a terrible heat in the land of Egypt, which burned up the flesh of man like <u>the sun in his circuit</u>, and it greatly oppressed the Egyptians."*

2 Enoch 12:2 is interesting, as it points to the sun going under the earth, *"Thus (the sun) revolves and goes, and rises under the heaven, and <u>its course goes under the earth</u> with the light of its rays incessantly."*

Scripture is earth focused, and it never declares that the earth is moving around the sun. Excuses have to be made to justify that the sun is not moving and that the earth is moving.

This chapter shows the congruency of Scripture, and that the geocentric globe earth model needs no excuses. The organic explanation, the literal view of Scripture, declares that the sun is moving and that the earth is fixed in its place.

Mainstream Christianity has embraced heliocentrism, not because there's Scriptural justification, but because men have declared it. And that's not good enough for me since we know that Satan's mission is to steal glory from the Creator, to deceive people about the creation, including the hopeless narrative of evolution which conveys that people have no value.

In my opinion, Christian ministries are promoting a fallacious cosmology based on man's reasoning rather than Bible exegesis. If you know of verses which declare that the sun is standing still in the universe or that the earth is moving through space, please use the book feedback page to let me know.

"God hath in these last days spoken unto us by his Son, whom he hath appointed heir of all things, by whom also he made the worlds; Who being the brightness of his glory, and the express image of his person, and upholding all things by the word of his power, when he had by himself purged our sins, sat down on the right hand of the Majesty on high; And, Thou, Lord, in the beginning hast laid the foundation of the earth; and the heavens are the works of thine hands."
Hebrews 1:2-3, 10

CHAPTER 46
Geocentric Earth Findings

In going through the 240 Bible verses that supposedly prove that the earth is flat with a dome over it; we can see that Scripture describes a geocentric universe, with a stationary earth and a sun that's moving in a circuit.

I'm not scientific, and I'm not an expert in astronomy, so I won't try to explain the design of the universe to you. What I will do is show you some information which has been hidden from the general population, even from college astronomy students. This is just a basic summary, and I'll provide links on the Resource Page so that you can investigate further.

When you think of the top names in the discussion; Copernicus, Galileo, Kepler, Newton, Einstein, etc., none of them ever provided scientific proof that the Earth revolves around the sun, they only gave a hypothesis.

While working at the request of Pope Leo X on improvements to the Julian calendar, Nicolaus Copernicus developed a system in which the earth moved. The concept was rejected for hundreds of years, but the Jesuits propped up many scientists who promote it, so that's it become the model which is prevalent.

Modern scientists admit that heliocentrism is the preferred system based on philosophical grounds, not scientific ones. Why would they prefer the heliocentric view over the geocentric model? Because a geocentric universe points to a Creator, and since they can't account for that, they side with the heliocentric view.

Before we get into the scientific findings, let's be clear about the geocentric model that makes sense.

You may have seen people proclaim to debunk the geocentric globe earth model, but most of them are basing that claim on the simplistic geocentric model, where the sun and earth are swapped, and all of the planets are orbiting around the earth. On that model, things such as the retrograde motion of planets, can't be explained.

But there's a more complex geocentric model that's been hidden, the Tychonic geocentric model.

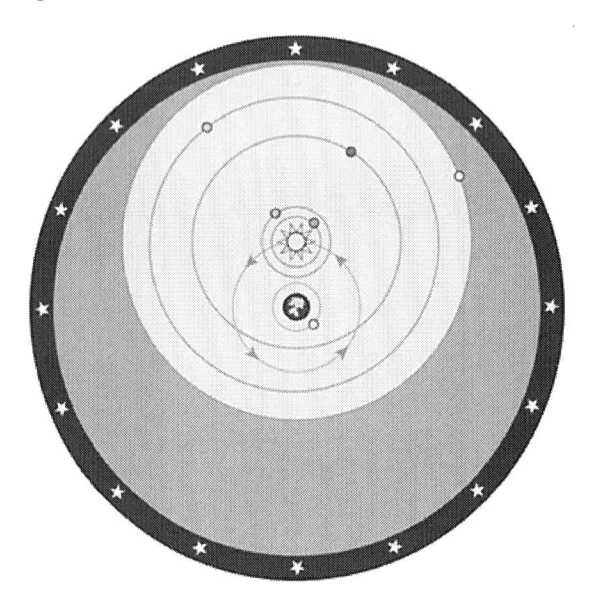

Tycho Brahe (1546-1601), a famous Danish astronomer, presented a different geocentric model which lined up with many of Copernicus's theories. He made the sun revolve around the earth, and the planets revolve around the sun.

This accounted for the geometry and distances that Copernicus had cited, and it allowed for retrograde motion of the planets. He also put Mercury and Venus at their correct distances from the sun, which corrected the Ptolemaic model.

I. Bernard Cohen, a famous U.S. physicist, wrote in his book *The Birth of a New Physics*: "There is no planetary observation by which we on earth can prove that the earth is moving in an orbit around the sun. Thus all Galileo's discoveries with the telescope can be accommodated to the system invented by Tycho Brahe just before Galileo began his observations of the heavens. In this Tychonic system, the planets Mercury, Venus, Mars, Jupiter, and Saturn move in orbits around the sun, while the sun moves in an orbit around the earth in a year. Furthermore, the daily rotation of the heavens is communicated to the sun and planets, so that the earth itself neither rotates nor revolves in an orbit." (1)

Tycho Brahe hired an apprentice named Johannes Kepler, but Brahe kept much of his research to himself until it was published. Contrary to Tycho Brahe, Kepler advocated for the Copernican heliocentric universe. It's interesting that Brahe died unexpectedly, and based on forensic evidence, he didn't die of natural causes but was systematically poisoned—most likely by his assistant, Kepler.

This allowed Kepler to access all of Brahe's notes to use for his Copernican explanations, and it effectively shut down the witness of the brilliant Tycho Brahe who advocated the geocentric globe earth model. Just two days after Tycho's death on October 24, 1601; Kepler was appointed as Brahe's successor as the Imperial Mathematician, perhaps as part of his reward.

Here's a summary of some notable experiments.

Attempts were made to prove that heliocentricity was true and geocentricity was false, but they failed. Instead, the experiments found that the Earth is standing still in space, which confronted the scientific community with devastating evidence that potentially destroyed the much revered Copernican Principle.

Flat-earthers ignorantly or deceptively cite these studies, but they don't point to a flat earth, rather they validate a geocentric globe earth.

In 1871, George Bidell Airy sought to prove that the earth is heliocentric, but instead, he proved that it's stationary.

To test the ether theory he had starlight travel through an empty telescope, and one filled with water slightly tipped to compensate for the estimated decrease in velocity of light through water and the estimated velocity of Earth. To his astonishment, the experiment indicated that the Earth is stationary, thus it's called *Airy's Failure*.

In 1877, the Michelson Morley Experiment established that the earth is stationary.

The most famous experiment was the Michelson-Morley Experiment. The New York Times described Professor Albert Michelson as *America's greatest physicist foremost in determining the velocity of light*. Astronomers proclaimed that the earth travels around the sun with a speed of more than eighteen miles a second, or 66,000 miles per hour. Working with Edward Morley, he carried out painstaking experiments to measure the velocity of the earth.

The theory was that light traveling east to west against the ether traveled slower than light traveling north to south. The result showed that there was slight motion, but not enough to indicate an orbiting Earth. What Airy found by examining starlight was now confirmed by Michelson with terrestrial light.

Michelson, who was dismayed at the results, said: *"This conclusion directly contradicts the explanation... which presupposes that the Earth moves."* (2)

Arthur Eddington gave a lecture in 1927, which is recorded in the book *The Nature of the Physical World*, in which he said about the Michelson-Morley experiment, *"There was just one alternative; the earth's true velocity through space might happen to have been nil."* (3)

Austrian-born physicist and recipient of the 1945 Nobel Prize for Physics, Wolfgang Pauli, said regarding the 1887 Michelson-Morley experiment and subsequent experiments: *"The failure of the many attempts to measure terrestrially any effects of the earth's motion* (4)

Science historian and physicist John D. Bernal stated: *"The Michelson-Morley experiment was the greatest negative result in the history of science."* In other words, they were expecting it to prove that the Earth was moving in space, but they proved the very opposite. (5)

In a book by Lincoln Barnett called *The Universe And Dr. Einstein*; which Albert Einstein endorsed by writing the foreword, it says: *"The experiment was tried again by Morley and by others, with the same conclusion: the apparent velocity of the Earth through the ether was zero."* (6) *"We can't feel our motion through space, nor has any physical experiment ever proved that the Earth actually is in motion."* (7)

Physicist G.J. Whitrow, in his book *The Structure and Evolution of the Universe* (1959), pointed out the implications of the Michelson-Morley experiment in refuting Nicolaus Copernicus. *"It is both amusing and instructive to speculate on what might have happened if such an experiment could have been performed in the sixteenth or seventeenth centuries when men were debating the rival merits of the Copernican and Ptolemaic systems. The result would surely have been interpreted as conclusive evidence for the immobility of the Earth, and therefore as a triumphant vindication of the Ptolemaic system and irrefutable falsification of the Copernican hypothesis."* (8)

Physicist Bernard Jaffe said in his book *Michelson and the Speed of Light* (1950): *"The data were almost unbelievable... There was only one other possible conclusion to draw – that the Earth is at rest."* (9)

Adolf Baker in his book *Modern Physics and Antiphysics* (1970) noted: *"Thus, the failure to observe different speeds of light at different times of the year suggested that the Earth must be 'at rest'... It was therefore the 'preferred' frame for measuring absolute motion in space."* (10)

I listed all of those quotes so that you can see the witness of the experts, who with one voice proclaimed that the Michelson-Morley experiment proved that the earth is at rest; because the enemy has hidden their witness. Astronomy students are not taught about the experiment or the great witness about it.

Many people have been used in an attempt to cover over the devastating results of the Michelson-Morley experiment; such as George Fitzgerald, Hendrick Lorentz, Arthur Eddington, and Albert Einstein.

Albert Einstein was used as controlled opposition.

In 1905, Einstein presented his *Special Theory of Relativity*, in which he used mathematics to appear to provide proof that the Michelson-Morley experiment was wrong. He proclaimed that the speed of light is constant and limited, and that there is no ether.

All of those statements have since been proven wrong. Mathematics works in theory but is proven or disproven by real-world experiments.

Albert Einstein is accused of being a Freemason celebrity scientist who promoted heliocentrism to keep humanity enslaved in ignorance. His Theory of Relativity was so purposefully complicated with sophistry that few people in the world were capable of understanding it.

The Sagnac Experiment debunked Einstein's Special Theory of Relativity.

In 1913, French physicist Georges Sagnac conducted an experiment using a ring interferometer which proved the existence of the ether, which Einstein's *Special Theory of Relativity* had discarded. And it showed that either space or Earth could be moving, proving Einstein's theory is wrong.

Albert Einstein countered with the General Theory of Relativity

In an attempt to cover over the evidence of Sagnac's Experiment, in 1915, Einstein presented his *General Theory of Relativity*, which supposedly accounted for gravity and inertial forces in a rotating reference frame.

But it inadvertently allowed for Earth orbiting the sun or vice versa because they're relative. The greater the centrifugal force, the faster light, or an object, can travel. The centrifugal force of the universe is huge, so it made it possible that the stars are rotating faster than 186,000 miles per second around a central point.

The Michelson-Gale experiment in 1925 confirmed the results obtained by Sagnac.

The Michelson–Gale–Pearson experiment was a modified version of the Michelson–Morley and the Sagnac Interferometer experiments. It served to confirm Sagnac's findings, once again proving the ether and showing that relativity is based on perspective.

Hebert Dingle invalidated Einstein's Theory Of Relativity.

Hebert Dingle promoted Einstein's theories for most of his life, and he was the world's foremost experts on the topic, writing the book, *The Special Theory Of Relativity*, which became the standard work in English. Then in 1959, after years of believing and promoting the theory, he found something wrong, he found a paradox.

He wanted access to scientific journals to prove out his theory, but he was denied. In 1972 he published a book called *Science At The Crossroads*, which proves that the *Theory of Relativity* is invalid. He found that movement was relative to the perspective of the observer; and that the theory doesn't prove which body is moving, the sun or earth.

Here's a snapshot of the comparison of the annual cycle. From earth, the perspective looks the same on both models.

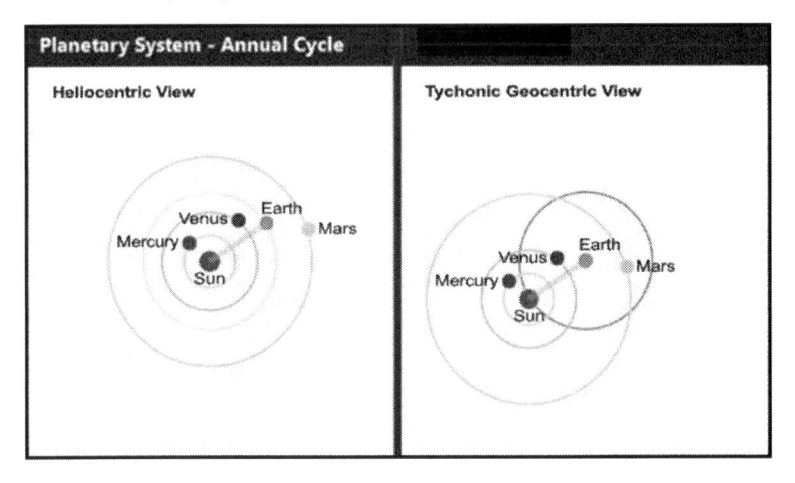

Planetary System - Annual Cycle

Heliocentric View | Tychonic Geocentric View

Here's a snapshot of the comparison of the daily cycle. Again from earth, the perspective looks the same on both models.

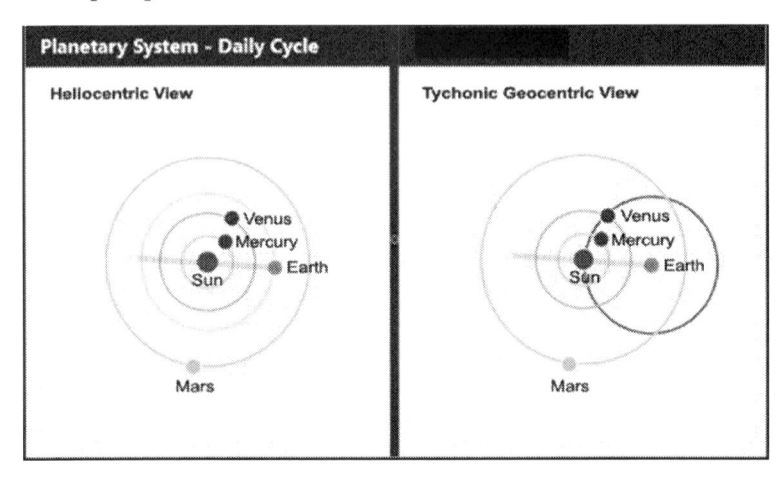

Planetary System - Daily Cycle

Heliocentric View | Tychonic Geocentric View

This could easily be hidden from most people, as they can't perceive the difference. Those who work in aviation, satellite technology, etc., would not be able to tell the difference, for the scientific principles that govern the earth work the same. Only high-level people at space agencies, such as NASA, would know the difference, allowing them to keep it hidden.

More evidence pointing to earth as the center of the universe has come to light in recent years, which has been hidden by the enemy.

Here's a summary from the book *Geocentrism 101 – An Introduction into the Science of Geocentric Cosmology* **by Robert A. Sungenis, Ph.D.**

Robert points out that few are aware that a year before he died Galileo renounced, quite dramatically, all his claims that the earth went around the sun.

In addition to Einstein's *General Theory of Relativity*, other theories of physics, such as *Newton's laws of motion* and *Mach's Principle*, say that a universe rotating around a fixed Earth is as scientifically valid as a rotating Earth in a fixed universe.

Every scientific proof for an Earth revolving around the sun has been discredited, and no experiment has provided proof that the Earth is moving.

The cosmic microwave radiation's dipole is aligned with the Earth's equator. The cosmic microwave radiation's quadrupole and octupole are aligned with the Earth-Sun ecliptic.

The distant quasars and radio galaxies are aligned with the Earth's equator and the North Celestial Pole. The Earth is in the center, and the mass of the surrounding universe is represented by the giant ball; showing how the signatures of the universe line up.

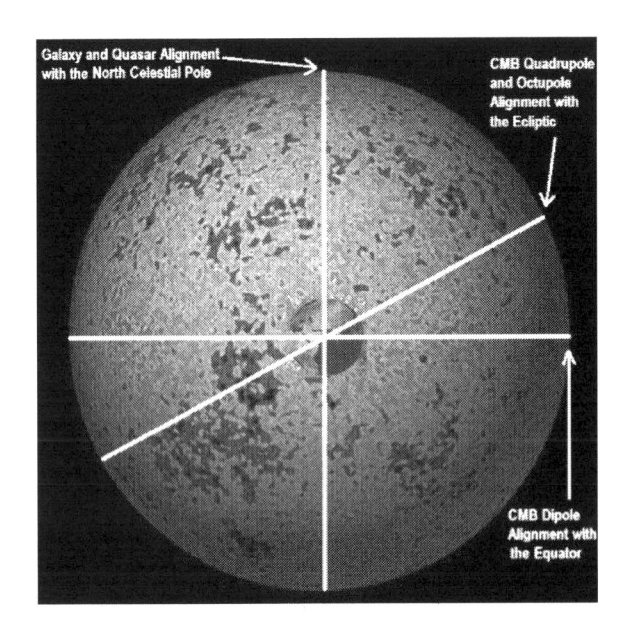

Essentially, three alignments provide the X, Y, and Z coordinates to place Earth in the very center of the known universe. Not only are the spin axes of galaxies and the cosmic microwave radiation aligned with Earth, but the distribution of galaxies shows that they lie mainly in concentric spheres around the Earth.

One important fact about the cosmic radiation alignment with the Earth-Sun ecliptic is that it fits perfectly with the Neo-Tychonic geocentric model. Since the Tychonic geocentric model has both the stars and the polarity of the cosmic microwave radiation aligned with the Sun, which all revolve around the fixed Earth, it is the only model that fits all of the cosmological data.

In his book *The Energy of Empty Space That Isn't Zero*, Physicist Lawrence Krauss said: *"But when you look at CMB map, you also see that the structure that is observed, is in fact, in a weird way, correlated with the plane of the earth around the sun. Is this Copernicus coming back to haunt us? That's crazy. We're looking out at the whole universe. That would say we are truly the center of the universe."* (11)

In his book *The Red Shift Hypothesis for Quasars: Is the Earth the Center of the Universe?*, astrophysicist Yetendra P. Varshni said: *"It is shown that the cosmological interpretation of the red shift in the spectra of quasars leads to yet another paradoxical result: namely, that the Earth is the center of the Universe. The Earth is indeed the center of the Universe. The arrangement of quasars on certain spherical shells is only with respect to the Earth. These shells would disappear if viewed from another galaxy or quasar. This means that the cosmological principle will have to go. Also, it implies that a coordinate system fixed to the Earth will be a preferred frame of reference in the Universe. Consequently, both the Special and General Theory of Relativity must be abandoned for cosmological purposes."* (12)

In his book *The Biggest Bangs*, astrophysicist Jonathan I. Katz said: *"No longer could astronomers hope that the Copernican dilemma would disappear with improved data. The data were in hand, and their implication inescapable: we are at the center of a spherically symmetric distribution of gamma-ray-burst sources, and this distribution has an outer edge."* (13)

It wasn't until scientific probes produced data about the radiation of the expanding universe, and the orientation of the quasars and radio galaxies; that researchers were able to see that all of those things were pointing back to Earth as the center of the universe. The cover-up of these experiments has been astounding, in that students in astronomy and other fields aren't even taught about them.

Here are some more notable quotes.

Albert Einstein stated, *"The possibility of solving these difficulties depends on the answer to the following question. Can we formulate physical laws so that they are valid for all coordinate systems, not only those moving uniformly, but also those moving quite arbitrarily, relative to each other? If this can be done, our difficulties will be over. We shall then be able to apply the laws of nature to any coordinate system.*

The struggle, so violent in the early days of science, between the views of Ptolemy and Copernicus would then be quite meaningless. Either coordinate system could be used with equal justification. The two sentences: "the sun is at rest and the Earth moves," or "the sun moves and the Earth is at rest," would simply mean two different conventions concerning two different coordinate systems." (14)

James Coleman, a theoretical physicist, in his book *Relativity for the Layman*, candidly stated, *"The easiest explanation was that the earth was fixed in the ether and that everything else in the universe moved with respect to the earth and the ether… Such an idea was not considered seriously, since it would mean in effect that our earth occupied the omnipotent position in the universes, with all the other heavenly bodies paying homage by moving around it."* (15)

George Ellis in an article titled *Thinking Globally, Acting Universally*, said, *"I can construct for you a spherically symmetrical universe with Earth at its center, and you cannot disprove it based on observations. You can only exclude it on philosophical grounds. In my view there is absolutely nothing wrong in that. What I want to bring into the open is the fact that we are using philosophical criteria in choosing our models. A lot of cosmology tries to hide that."* (16)

There's a lot of compelling scientific evidence that the Earth is indeed at the center of the universe, but the enemy has done a masterful job of covering it over, to push the hopeless teaching of evolution which undermines the Genesis account in the Bible.

It's very interesting and telling, that shortly after these findings were published in 2013, the flat earth theory was aggressively pushed on YouTube and Facebook; seemingly to try to cover over the evidence, and to cause people to dismiss anyone who teaches that the Earth is geocentric.

Flat-earthers believe that the enemy has created a deception to hide the design of the universe, to hide the Creator. I believe that is true, but the enemy's deception points to the geocentric globe earth model; which is largely ignored both by flat earthers and heliocentric globe-earth defenders. Taking into consideration that the enemy controls the major space agencies, I think that it's possible that they're giving false information to hide the truth.

Johann Wolfgang von Goethe (1749-1832), a German writer and statesman, said this about the damage that Copernicus had caused: *"Among all the (scientific) discoveries and (new) convictions, not a single one has resulted in deeper influence on the human spirit than the doctrine of Copernicus. The Copernican revolution did indeed eventually bequeath to modernity an essentially beginningless, structureless, purposeless, and godless cosmos, in which the Earth and man henceforth appear as cosmic specks, meaningless accidents wandering aimlessly about in the void. All coherence—and all comfort—was indeed gone."* (17)

Christian astronomer Gerardus D. Bouw, PhD, in his book *Geocentricity: Christianity in the Woodshed*, notes: *"All of these physicists (and there is not a geocentric Christian in the bunch) conclude that there is no detectable, experimental difference between having the Earth spin diurnally on an axis as well as orbit the sun once a year, or having the universe rotate about the Earth once a day and possessing a wobble centered on the sun which carries the planets and stars about the Earth once a year. In none of these models would the universe fly apart, nor would a stationary satellite fall to the earth. In every one of these models the astronauts on the moon would still see all sides of the Earth in the course of 24 hours, the Foucault pendulum would still swing exactly the same way as we see it in museums, and the Earth's equator would still bulge. In other words, each of these effects is due to either the centrifugal force, Coriolis force, or some combination of the two, and can be totally explained in any geocentric model."* (17)

Nikola Tesla was a brilliant scientist, who filed more than three hundred patents during his eighty-six years of life, and his inventions helped pave the way for alternating current (AC), electric motors, radios, fluorescent lights, lasers, remote controls, among many other things. About Einstein's Theory of Relativity, he said, *"The theory wraps all these errors and fallacies and clothes them in magnificent mathematical garb which fascinates, dazzles and makes people blind to the underlying errors. The theory is like a beggar clothed in purple whom ignorant people take for a king. Its exponents are very brilliant men, but they are metaphysicists rather than scientists."* (18)

Stephen Hawking said, *"So which is real, the Ptolemaic or the Copernican system? Although it is not uncommon for people to say that Copernicus proved Ptolemy wrong, that is not true. As in the case of our normal view versus that of the goldfish, one can use either picture as a model of the universe, for our observations of the heavens can be explained by assuming either the earth or the sun to be at rest."* (19)

The enemy has covered over this evidence and pushed the heliocentric model so that they can push their evolution agenda and hide the Creator. Now you see why I believe that the real deception of the enemy is the geocentric globe earth model and that the flat earth theory has been promoted to cover over the truth.

Can I scientifically prove that the earth is geocentric? No, but as you've seen, the geocentric universe is the only model which requires no excuses, as it's fully congruent with Scripture.

Evil men control the world in these end times, and I don't blindly trust what NASA and the scientific community tells me; for I know that they're lying about the age of the earth and evolution.

Scripture does not describe a flat earth with a dome over it, so we can see that the enemy is pushing an agenda to hide the truth, and to discredit believers.

CHAPTER 47
The Deception About Earth's Orientation

Flat-earthers proclaim that before the heliocentric model was pushed by Copernicus, most people believed that the earth is flat; but that's not true. They believed in a geocentric globe earth, not a flat earth.

In the fourth century BC, two influential Greek philosophers, Plato, and his student Aristotle wrote works based on the geocentric globe earth model. In the second century AD, Claudius Ptolemy of Alexandria devised a complex system of *'epicycles'* to account for retrograde (going backward) motion of the planets on the model.

To understand why the deception of the heliocentric universe was created, we have to look back to how Satan has fought against Messiah and His saints. In Daniel's prophecies, he describes four beast kingdoms which consecutively reign in power until Messiah returns; Babylon > Medo-Persia > Greece > Rome.

The fourth beast kingdom of Rome was in power during Messiah's ministry, and it was used to desolate the city of Jerusalem, the temple and many Jews, in 70 AD. Satan used the Roman Emperors to try to wipe out the early church, killing millions of saints during the first few centuries; but Messiah's assembly of saints grew stronger. HalleluYah!

As the Roman Empire was declining from bloody civil wars, economic strife, famine, and pestilence; Satan changed his strategy and sought to create a 'christian' church of his own, which has the veneer of the true faith but misleads people with a false salvation message, and concepts which are contrary to Scripture.

If you're Catholic, my intention isn't to offend you, but you need to know the truth so that you're in right standing before the Father. Prophecy fulfillment and historical evidence show that the enemy formed the Roman Catholic Church to seek to destroy Messiah's true assembly of saints from within. Messiah has commanded His people to come out of the teachings of the *harlot* church.

At its core, the doctrine of the Papal Church is based on the Babylonian mystery religion of sun god worship, which is why there's an Egyptian obelisk (a phallic symbol of the Egyptian sun god Ra) erected in the middle of a sun wheel, in St. Peter's Square.

It's why there's a massive sun symbol inside of St. Peter's Basilica, which is filled with the statues of pagan gods, who they gave the names of the apostles and Mary. It's why they raise up a round Eucharist wafer (which symbolizes the sun god) and cause people to revere it. They proclaim that it becomes the body of Christ, but the 'christ' that they're symbolizing is the supposed incarnate son of the Babylonian moon goddess Semiramis, Tammuz.

Tammuz is the pagan christ child that the Israelites were worshiping, as they were idolatrous worshippers of the sun god. *"He said also unto me, Turn thee yet again, and thou shalt see greater abominations that they do. Then he brought me to the door of the gate of the LORD'S house which was toward the north; and, behold, there sat women weeping for Tammuz."* Ezekiel 8:13-14

Through the Roman bishops and Emperors, the counterfeit christian church was set up. The saints had been harshly persecuted by Rome for hundreds of years, so when Emperor Constantine ended the persecutions, the Roman leaders sought to cause people to compromise their beliefs and join with the Roman church. Sadly, many apostatized and *fell away* from the true faith.

After the last Western Roman Emperor was removed from power in 476 AD, the Roman Popes took authority over the Roman Empire. As their power and influence increased, their proclamations became more blasphemous; as they proclaimed to be god, to be Jesus Christ in the flesh, and to forgive sins. The Popes created many concepts which are contrary to Scripture.

During the Dark Ages, the Popes banned and burned the Scriptures, and persecuted the saints who believed the Scriptures over their teachings. They tortured the saints to try to get them to convert to Catholicism. Google images of *'catholic torture devices'* and you'll see their demonic brutal torture devices.

During the Protestant Reformation, the saints defended Scripture over the teachings of the Popes. They exposed the falsehood of the doctrine that Catholic Popes and priests can forgive sins, that salvation is through the sacraments, that Mary is the intercessor to the Father, etc. The Reformers testified that the teachings of the Popes are anti-Messiah.

The Jesuits of Rome were empowered in the 16th century to counter the Protestants regarding ecclesiastic matters, and to deceive the world about many things. The Jesuits are not just a priestly order, but a military power, which is led by the Superior General, who is referred to as the *Black Pope*.

The founder of the Jesuit order, Ignatius Loyola; used self-flagellation, spent time in caves on spiritual retreats, and studied the principles of the Satanic Egyptian Kabbalah; to develop his evil 'religious' beliefs. The *Jesuit Spiritual Exercises* subject Jesuit priests to meditations, prayers, and other contemplative practices; which causes them to become mind-controlled, with unquestioned obedience to the orders of the Superior General.

Here's part of the Jesuit Oath which exposes their evil guiding 'principles': *I furthermore promise and declare that I will, when opportunity present, make and wage relentless war, secretly or openly, against all heretics, Protestants, and Liberals, as I am directed to do, to extirpate and exterminate them from the face of the whole earth; and that I will spare neither age, sex or condition; and that I will hang, waste, boil, flay, strangle and bury alive these infamous heretics, rip up the stomachs and wombs of their women and crush their infants' heads against the walls, in order to annihilate forever their execrable race. That when the same cannot be done openly, I will secretly use the poisoned cup, the strangulating cord, the steel of the poniard or the leaden bullet, regardless of the honor, rank, dignity, or authority of the person or persons, whatever may be their condition in life, either public or private, as I at any time may be directed so to do by any agent of the Pope or Superior of the Brotherhood of the Holy Faith, of the Society of Jesus.*

French military genius Napoleon Bonaparte told us exactly who the Jesuits are: *"The Jesuits are a MILITARY organization, not a religious order. Their chief is a general of an army, not the mere father abbot of a monastery. And the aim of this organization is power – power in its most despotic exercise – absolute power, universal power, power to control the world by the volition of a single man* (the office of the Superior General of the Jesuits). *Jesuitism is the most absolute of despotisms; and at the same time the greatest and most enormous of abuses. Their society is by nature dictatorial, and therefore it is the irreconcialable enemy of all constituted authority. Every act, every crime, however atrocious, is a meritorious work, if committed for the interest of the Society of Jesus, or by the order of the general."* (1)

Messiah warned, *"Beware of false prophets, which come to you in sheep's clothing, but inwardly they are ravening wolves."* Matthew 7:15

That describes the Jesuit leaders 'to a T,' as they dress and act like Christian priests (*lamb-like*), but they're really wolves who serve Satan (the *dragon*).

Interestingly, the third Jesuit Superior General from 1565-1572, Francesco Borgia, said: *"We came in like lambs and will rule like wolves. We shall be expelled like dogs and return like eagles."*

The Strong's Greek Dictionary word for *"false prophet"* is 5578 *pseudoprophetes* from 5571 and 4396; which means *a spurious prophet, i.e., pretended foreteller or a religious impostor.* Greek word 5571 *pseudes* means *untrue, i.e., erroneous, deceitful, wicked:—false, liar.*

The Superior General is exactly that, a *false priest*, a *religious impostor*; who doesn't serve Yahuah or Messiah, but rather he wickedly serves Satan. He hypocritically feigns to be a priest, in order the better to covertly make war with Messiah and His saints. Jesuit priests carried out the *Inquisition* and tortured and killed the saints if they didn't convert to Catholicism.

A one-man antichrist can't just magically control the world. The militant Jesuit Order, who have historically been kicked out of many countries, including primarily Catholic ones; has covertly set up a vast organization of people who control most of the world.

The Jesuits founded the Bavarian Illuminati through Adam Weishaupt; they infiltrated Freemasonry to illuminate people's minds, to use the leaders for their agenda; they use the Rothschild family to steal the wealth of nations via their fraudulent central banks, such as the Federal Reserve bank, through which they print money out of thin air and charge interest on it; and they control many people groups and the major corporations; in an attempt to push the world into a Satanic One World Government.

At the lower levels of the Jesuit Order are priests who are oblivious to the deeds of the leaders; who are used to spread the false gospel of Catholicism around the world, and to do works of service in order to give Jesuits a good reputation.

It's through these Jesuit leaders that many deceptions have been inspired. The Popes had banned and burned the Scriptures during the Dark Ages so that they could control the message. But during the Protestant Reformation, the saints were given the manuscripts, and they translated them into the common languages, and with the advent of the printing press, the printed Bible was spread around the world; proclaiming the true salvation message, which exposes the Popes' teachings as anti-Messiah.

The Jesuits can't stop Bibles from being printed, so since the 16th century, they've worked hard to corrupt Bibles. They used heretics Brook Foss Westcott and Fenton John Anthony Hort, who don't believe in the deity of Messiah; to create the *Westcott and Hort Greek New Testament* in 1811 and the *English Revised Version Bible* in 1815; which has led to more corrupt Bible versions such as the *New International Version (NIV)*; all of which are missing many words and verses which validate Messiah's deity.

Knowing the role of the Jesuits, let's focus on how they've worked to counter beliefs that the universe is geocentric. Up until the 16th century, the scientific community believed that the globe earth is the center of the universe. Believers understood that the language of Scripture is geocentric.

WorldsLastChance.com, which promotes the flat earth theory, states, *"Prior to Copernicus, most well educated people believed in the Ptolemaic model of the universe, which placed a flat, enclosed earth at the center of the universe."* That's not true, as Ptolemy taught a geocentric universe model, with the sun and planets revolving around the globe earth.

Ptolemy did not teach that the earth is flat and enclosed by a dome! Flat-earthers deceive people by proclaiming that their model is geocentric, but it's not!

Knowing that Satan's goal is to cause people to reject the Scriptures and the Creator, and to steal worship away from Him; he contrived the heliocentric model of the universe to act as the vehicle to push the evolution narrative, which is contrary to the Genesis account of creation, and serves to undermine the validity of the Scriptures.

Enter Nicolas Copernicus, a Polish Catholic who belonged to the Third Order of St. Dominic. He studied astronomy in his pursuit of a career in the Catholic Church. He learned that Aristarchus of Samos, a Greek philosopher in the third century BC, proposed that the sun was the center of the universe, not the earth. Helios is the Greek sun god, so the sun-centered model of the universe was named the heliocentric system.

Catholic bishops urged Copernicus to submit his manuscripts for publication, as they wanted the heliocentric view to be pushed, but he delayed until he was near death. He waited so that he didn't have to face the backlash of his contemporaries who believed that the earth is geocentric. A completed, published copy of his book was placed in his hands shortly before his death in May 1543. Copernicus dedicated his book, *Revolutions of the Heavenly Bodies*, to Pope Paul III.

Here's some key excerpts from the dedication, which are very telling: *I can easily conceive, most Holy Father, that as soon as some people learn that in this book which I have written concerning the revolutions of the heavenly bodies, I ascribe certain motions to the Earth, <u>they will cry out at once that I and my theory should be rejected</u>.*

Accordingly, when I considered in my own mind <u>how absurd a performance it must seem to those who know that the judgment of many centuries has approved the view that the Earth remains fixed as center in the midst of the heavens</u>, if I should, on the contrary, assert that the Earth moves. Therefore, when I considered this carefully, the contempt which I had to fear because of <u>the novelty and apparent absurdity of my view, nearly induced me to abandon utterly the work I had begun</u>. (2)

Those are the words of someone who published a theory which is against his good conscience, who was stating that he was pressured to complete this work, which he knew was absurd.

The Protestant Reformers not only witnessed against Rome's false gospel; but they opposed the concept of a heliocentric universe as well, as it's contrary to Scripture.

In a Table Talk discussion with Martin Luther, the topic of Copernicus came up, to which Luther replied, *"So it goes now. Whoever wants to be clever must agree with nothing that others esteem. He must do something of his own. This is what that fellow does who wishes to turn the whole of astronomy upside down. Even in these things that are thrown into disorder I believe the Holy Scriptures, for Joshua* (10:12) *commanded the sun to stand still, and not the earth."* (3)

Pastor Dean Odle cites this quote from Martin Luther on his website to counter the heliocentric earth model, which he says proves that the earth is flat. But that's intellectually dishonest as Luther was defending the geocentric globe earth.

Protestant Reformer John Calvin also opposed Copernican heliocentrism, warning his followers against those who asserted, *"that the sun does not move and that it is the earth that moves and turns."* Such persons were motivated by *"a spirit of bitterness, contradiction, and faultfinding;"* possessed by the devil, they aimed *"to pervert the order of nature."* (4)

Joseph F. MacDonnell, a Jesuit historian, in his book *Companions of Jesuits: A Tradition of Collaboration* (1995) declared, *"It is a challenge for historians to find a single significant scientist of the sixteenth, seventeenth and eighteenth centuries who was not in some way involved with Jesuits and their colleagues: as students, as teachers, as relatives, as collaborators, as adversaries, as rivals or simply as personal friends."* (5)

One would think that Jesuit priests would only be focused on ecclesiastical matters, but that is far from the truth. They are actively involved in the field of science, especially in astronomy, which allows them to control the message. To see a list of well-known Jesuit astronomers, Google the search term *"Wikipedia list of catholic clergy scientists."*

Christopher Clavius (1537–1612), a leading Jesuit astronomer in the sixteenth century, incorporated Copernican mathematical models in the Jesuit curriculum and was the principal scholar behind the creation of the Gregorian calendar.

Galileo Galilei (1564-1642), an Italian astronomer, has been called the *"father of observational astronomy,"* the *"father of modern physics,"* the *"father of the scientific method,"* and the *"father of modern science."*

Galileo was close friends with Christopher Clavius, who no doubt had a great influence on his explanations. When Galileo published his book *Starry Messenger* (1610), Jesuit astronomers confirmed his discoveries. Galileo's interest in *falling bodies* originated with a Jesuit named Niccolo Cabeo (1586-1650).

Another Jesuit, Honore Fabri (1608-1688), was the first to explain Galileo's experiment demonstrating equal time for falling bodies. We can see the direct relationship of Galileo's explanations and the support of the Jesuits.

You've already read about Johannes Kepler, who was the assistant of Tycho Brahe until Brahe died under mysterious circumstances.

When Kepler became destitute and didn't have a telescope of his own, a Jesuit mathematician named Paul Guldin (1577-1643) encouraged fellow Jesuit Niccolo Zucchi (1586-1670) to provide Kepler with a telescope. Kepler was so grateful that he dedicated his book to Guldin.

"To the very reverend Father Paul Guldin, priest of the Society of Jesus, venerable and learned man, beloved patron. <u>There is hardly anyone at this time with whom I would rather discuss matters of astronomy than with you</u>. Even more of a pleasure to me, therefore, was the greeting from your reverence which was delivered to me by members of your order who are here. Fr. Zucchi could not have entrusted this most remarkable gift – I speak of the telescope – to anyone whose effort in his connection pleases me more than yours. Since you are the first to tell me that this jewel is to become my property, I think you should receive from me the first literary fruit of the joy that I gained from trial of this gift." (6)

When Kepler was unable to get his Almanac printed, the Jesuit College at Ingolstadt took control of getting it published. Kepler clearly had an intimate relationship with the Jesuits.

Georges Henri Joseph Édouard Lemaître (1894-1966), was a Jesuit trained Belgian priest, mathematician, astronomer, and professor of physics at the Catholic University of Louvain. He's the father of the *big bang theory*. He was a close friend of Albert Einstein, perhaps his handler, as Einstein was used to counter teachings of a fixed earth and the geocentric universe.

Interestingly, in 2014, Jesuit Pope Francis professed support of the big bang theory and evolution, saying: *"The Big Bang, that today is considered to be the origin of the world, does not contradict the creative intervention of God; on the contrary, it requires it. Evolution in nature is not in contrast with the notion of (divine) creation because evolution requires the creation of the beings that evolve."* (7)

Jesuit Pierre Teilhard de Chardin (1881-1955) was the creator of the *Piltdown man hoax*, in which a small human skull was mated to the jaw of an orangutan. One would imagine that the hoax of the evolution theory would be promoted by an atheist, but here we see that it is the Jesuits.

The Jesuits brought former Nazi Germany scientists to the USA during *Operation Paperclip*, some who were used to lead NASA, to create an entity which would allow them to control the message about the design of the universe. Though many countries and universities have observatories; NASA is the world-wide authority in making statements about discoveries, about lunar missions, about photographs, etc.

Many of the major telescopes and observatories in the world are owned and controlled by the Jesuits. They control the Vatican Advanced Technology Telescope (VATT) on Mount Graham in southeast Arizona. The Large Binocular Telescope is one of the world's largest and most powerful optical telescopes.

Scripture describes a geocentric earth, not a heliocentric one. The saints believed that the earth is geocentric until the Jesuits propped up astronomers who taught the heliocentric system. They pushed their deception until it has become the accepted model, despite the lack of evidence.

Mainstream scientists declare that the earth is in a heliocentric universe, but that doesn't mean that it's true, for we know that the enemy seeks to deceive people about the Creator, to steal glory away from Him.

The Copernican Revolution removed the earth from its special place, in the center of the glorious sphere of the forty-eight constellations, and reduced it to the status of another planet that revolves around the sun.

The concept of heliocentrism was the beginning of the assault on the authority of Scripture. It is the key vehicle to push the evolution agenda, which invalidates the authority of the Genesis narrative and steals glory from the Creator. Today, most pastors, seminaries, denominations, creation ministries, etc.; promote the heliocentric model without any Scriptural justification.

I list geocentric research websites and books on the book Resource Page if you want to do more research.

I'll finish this chapter by noting something that's really peculiar. Some of the key people who expose the Jesuit leaders as the enemy of Messiah and His saints, and the foe of humanity; now promote the flat earth theory. This includes Alan Lamont, Eric Jon Phelps, Johnny Cirucci, and the World's Last Chance website. I think that's very significant. Are they controlled opposition?

They know that the Jesuits have created many deceptions to fool believers and the whole world. They know that before the 16th century, believers understood that the Bible describes a geocentric globe earth, and the scientific community believed that the universe is geocentric. So they're lying when they proclaim that most people believed that the earth is flat.

They know that some of the Protestant Reformers, such as Martin Luther, John Calvin, and Philipp Melanchthon; condemned the heliocentric model of Copernicus, and proclaimed that Scripture describes a geocentric globe earth; yet these people lie and use quotes from these Reformers as supposed flat earth proof.

They know that experiments have been carried out which prove that the globe earth is not moving, yet they lie and cite those experiments as supposed proof that the earth is flat. And they know that the Jesuits control NASA and the scientific world.

So how do these people believe in the flat earth theory, when all of the evidence points to a geocentric globe earth? Are they controlled opposition who teach a lot of truth about the Jesuits, to get people to trust them; but who really work for the Jesuits, to provide false explanations such as the flat earth theory?

Ironically, Johnny Cirucci accused me of working for the Jesuits and promoting their false cosmology. A sociopath accuses you of doing the very thing that they are guilty of themselves. Since the Jesuits promote the heliocentric model, not the geocentric model, his accusation is without merit.

Recall Johnny Cirucci's statement about me, *"You either work for them (the Jesuits) or are demonically deluded. The REALITY of our cosmology undoes the Jesuit discrediting of Scripture and YOU aid them to shore it up. You either consciously wish to shore up the false Jesuit cosmology to discredit the Bible or you're critically, tragically attached to the lie…which doesn't say much for your Walk. We'll see soon enough who was on the side of Christ and His Word. YOU'RE A FRAUD."*

This book proves out who is working for the Jesuits or is demonically deluded. It proves out what Scripture teaches and exposes the Jesuit's flat-earth deception. And it proves who is on the side of Messiah and His Word, and who is the fraud.

This book exposes the flat-earth leaders, for they're deceiving people about the shape of the earth and the orientation of the universe. Whether they're doing it on purpose or they're just ignorant, won't change the fact that they will stand before their righteous Judge to account for their false teachings.

They and all flat-earthers are effectively hiding the real deception of the Jesuits, about the orientation of the universe. By promoting the flat-earth theory, they're causing people to reject the geocentric globe earth model, so they're complicit in the enemy's deception.

CHAPTER 48
The Mindset Of A Flat-Earther

There are many deceptions in these end-times, which creates distrust in governmental institutions, the mainstream media, large corporations, etc. Many people are waking up to the crimes of the elite and are exposing them online; via websites, Facebook, and YouTube. This creates a culture where people don't trust anything and have paranoid tendencies.

The gap between people who can see the many deceptions, and those who are apathetic and ignorant, gets wider every day. This causes people to seek like-minded groups on social media because family and friends are not seeing how they're being misled.

Believers know that the scientific community is deceiving the world, that they're covering over the truth and they're pushing the enemy's narrative of evolution; which steals glory from the Creator.

This makes people ripe for the flat earth deception because it provides a narrative that points to a Designer, it supposedly exposes the deception of the government and the scientific community, and it gives people a movement where like-minded people can join forces.

It gives people a platform to be seen as an 'expert,' as they speak on YouTube discussions and at flat-earth conferences. And it allows the leaders to make money; by selling books and other flat-earth products, and from YouTube ad royalties.

Not only do Christian flat-earthers believe that the leaders of the world have deceived people about the shape of the earth, but they believe that pastors have been complicit, as they agree with the heliocentric model.

What the enemy has done is create high production value videos such as Eric Dubay's *'200 Proofs Earth is Not a Spinning Ball.'* It has sharp graphics, dramatic background music, and authoritative narration. Eric gives many talking points that program people's minds, such as *"the horizon always rises to meet our eyes."* Ironically, Eric says that the flat earth theory has been called *"an ignorant, unscientific world view."*

At first, people may be skeptical about the flat earth, but after watching video after video, their belief evolves. As they see others commenting on the videos, they come to believe that they're part of a special community, which has secret knowledge that's been hidden from most people.

Through the repetition of watching flat earth videos, the talking points are embedded into their minds. They become so convinced that it gets to the point that you can provide absolute evidence that the earth is not flat, but they can't see or admit the evidence which is contrary to their belief. This is called *cognitive dissonance.*

Sometimes people hold a core belief that is very strong, that when they're presented with evidence which is against that belief, the new evidence cannot be accepted because it creates a feeling that is extremely uncomfortable. Because it's so important to protect the core belief, they will rationalize, ignore, and deny anything that doesn't fit with that core belief. This is why people get upset when their strongly held beliefs are challenged.

A great example of this is when Nathan Roberts and Pastor Dean Odle captured video of the view from Fairhope to Mobile, Alabama; declaring that it proves the flat earth and that *the globe is dead*. But the video proved the opposite; as the bottom four floors of the targeted building, and the elevated roadway in the foreground of the building are missing.

After admitting on the video that the bottom part of the building is missing, Nathan made excuses, that it's due to the *law of perspective* and *haze*, which is ridiculous. If the earth were flat, then there's nothing to hide the bottom four floors. In the video, we can see the top of the water, and we can see the building, so haze is not blocking our view. Nathan can't see or admit evidence which proves that the earth is flat, because his whole world is based on it.

On a National Geographic video called *'Flat Earth vs. Round Earth'* the Independent Investigations Group ran a test at the Salton Sea in California, with a boat moving away from them which had a sign with red and black horizontal stripes.

Mark Sargent and other flat-earthers were present during the test. When it was proved that the stripes on the sign disappeared bottom first, proving that the earth and water were curving; Mark said that it's due to *'heat.'* He either has cognitive dissonance, or he's a deceiver because the evidence is clear to see.

It's amazing that flat-earthers can witness a test which proves the curvature, but instead of it opening their eyes, they make up excuses. Why? Because admitting that there's curvature would put a crack in their flat earth dome theory.

There's a mental bias when it comes to the flat earth, as people want to believe that there's a designed universe that proves that there's a Creator. It gives them comfort, security, and it affirms their faith. And there's a bias because not only do they think that the world has been deceived, but that most believers are deceived about what Scripture is proclaiming. And that makes them feel very special.

When I attended the Flat Earth Conference debate between flat-earther Rob Skiba and geocentrist Robert Sungenis in November 2018; I heard someone proudly proclaim that "*we're pioneers*" and those around him smiled and nodded their heads in agreement.

There are many deceptions in the world, so it's easy to believe that everything is fake. Mark Sargent says that *"the only reason that NASA was founded was to keep this (the flat earth) under wraps."* What if one of NASA's agendas is to hide that the earth is geocentric? Are Mark Sargent and other flat earth leaders controlled opposition, who get paid to hide that the earth is geocentric?

Those who attended the Flat Earth International Conference told a reporter something notable, that *"they had been kicked out of churches, or lost jobs with churches, or suffered broken relationships with family members"* due to their beliefs. They're emotionally invested in the flat earth, so to find out that it's not flat would rock their world.

Amazingly, flat-earthers can't see that the Tychonic geocentric globe earth model proves that there's a Designer and Creator, it proves that the earth isn't flying through space, and it proves that there's a massive deception, but they don't even consider it as an option. By ignorantly proclaiming that the earth is flat, they've effectively hidden the geocentric globe earth model.

The enemy has created a deception, as two of the three models (flat earth, geocentric, heliocentric) are wrong. Any debate about the design of the universe should include the Tychonic geocentric earth, but both flat-earthers and heliocentric globe-earthers ignore it. Just as flat-earthers are biased in their view of Scripture and evidence, so too are Christian ministries who, without Scriptural justification, promote the heliocentric globe earth model.

I believe that the enemy is promoting the flat earth movement to discredit scientific findings which point to the earth being at the center of the universe, as it causes people to reject not only the flat earth model but anything to do with the geocentric model. And it also harms the reputation of believers who promote the flat earth.

CHAPTER 49
Your Conclusion

This conclusion is about what you saw in the explanations. I've addressed the major points that flat-earthers make about Scripture, and have shown that none of them prove that the earth is flat with a dome over it and that some of the verses that they cite describe a geocentric globe earth.

Flat-earthers, I've asked you throughout this book, how do you justify these verses being on the flat earth list? Did you see that it's not a case of flat-earthers having 240 verses and globe earthers having none? Did you see that many of the verses that are cited can also point to a geocentric globe earth? Is it possible that the enemy has pushed the flat-earth model to cover over the geocentric globe earth model?

For people who believe that the universe is heliocentric, I asked you to keep an open mind, to look at what Scripture is proclaiming. How do you justify a heliocentric universe based on Scripture? Is it possible that the enemy has pushed the heliocentric model to deceive people with their evolution doctrine?

My purpose in writing this book is to prove that Scripture does not describe a flat earth with a dome over it, and I feel that I've accomplished that goal. What I learned while doing research is that Scripture describes a geocentric universe, in which the sun is moving in a circuit, and the globe earth is fixed in place.

If the universe is geocentric, then part of what flat-earthers believe is true; that the earth is not flying through space at 66,600 MPH.

If this is true, then it's a huge revelation, and we can see why the enemy would take steps to cover it up; including controlling the scientific community and pushing the flat earth theory.

Flat earthers deny that gravity exists because it's based on a globe-earth, so it's ironic that the Bible mentions *"gravity"* twice.

"One that ruleth well his own house, having his children in subjection with all gravity." 1 Timothy 3:4

"In all things shewing thyself a pattern of good works: in doctrine shewing uncorruptness, gravity, sincerity, sound speech, that cannot be condemned; that he that is of the contrary part may be ashamed, having no evil thing to say of you." Titus 2:7-8

The word *"gravity"* is pointing to *honesty*. The Strong's Greek word is 4587 *semnotes,* which means; *venerableness, probity: gravity, honesty.*

1 Timothy 2:2 gives an example of the Greek word *semnotes* being used for honesty. *"For kings, and for all that are in authority; that we may lead a quiet and peaceable life in all godliness and honesty."*

Why do I bring up the word *gravity*, which points to *honesty*? Because there's no *gravity* in Nathan Roberts' explanations, for he has been intellectually dishonest. You've seen the nonsensical statements that he makes to try to justify the flat earth model. You've seen how he takes verse after verse out of their proper context, to proclaim that they're flat-earth verses.

Honest people don't list five Bible verses that are about John the Baptist *"preparing the way for Messiah, to make His way straight,"* as flat earth proofs!

Honest people don't ignore the context of 2 Samuel 11:11, which is about Uriah's army sleeping in tents in an *"open field,"* just to be able to proclaim that *"the Bible says flat earth."*

It was a shameful premise that David tried to get Uriah to sleep with his wife, to try to cover over his sin of adultery; and it's a shameful premise that Nathan lists this as a flat earth proof.

So let's bring this full circle. Recall these quotes from Nathan Roberts, which were directed at me.

"For anyone to state otherwise, and even publish a website, against this biblical truth is quite insane. You have to delude God's Word to believe in anything other than a stationary and flat earth when reading God's Word in CONTEXT…which you seem to have a difficult time doing.

You are preach FALSE doctrine in a VERY BOLD way. For those who are attempting to research this topic from a Biblical perspective your website doesn't do any justice to God's Word, it is an embarrassment and a shame.

The confusion you espouse on your website gets absorbed by unsuspecting researchers and then they bring that confusion into their relationships, and that is what causes the division. **Your work is a complete and utter disservice to unity that should be found in God's Word.** *By the way…did you know that water ALWAYS finds level, I know…its profound.*

You need to take this website down, repent, and publicly apologize to all people you have steered wrong…otherwise, you are nothing more than a wolf in sheep's clothing from my standpoint. May God bless your obedience."

I believe that I've proven that it is Nathan who has deluded our Heavenly Father's Word, who has taken verses out of context, whose explanations are a complete and utter disservice to the community of believers.

I believe that I've proven that it's Nathan who should repent, publically apologize, take his website down, and stop selling his books. May our Heavenly Father bless his obedience!

I pray that this book has opened your eyes and exposed the true context of the 240 verses that flat-earthers cite. More than that, I hope that you now see how Scripture and the *Gospel In The Stars* point to a globe earth, for in them is the glory of our Heavenly Father's redemption story. HalleluYah!

Now that you've read the whole book, what's your conclusion? You're welcome to share your perspective of the explanations on this page. **FlatEarthDeception.com/feedback**

If you disagree with me, please provide a Scriptural defense of your belief, so that can have an honest discussion.

May our Heavenly Father bless you and keep you, as you search out Scriptural truth!

David

"I Jesus have sent mine angel to testify unto you these things in the churches. I am the root and the offspring of David, and the bright and morning star."
Revelation 22:16

Appendix

My purpose in writing this book is to debunk that the Bible says that the earth is flat with a dome over it, and I believe that I've accomplished that goal. But if you've believed that the earth is flat, then I realize that this may create a conflict in your mind because you've seen explanations which seem to prove a flat earth.

To help you, I created a free Research Guide to share some insights that I learned during my investigation, which helped me see how people are misrepresenting things to skew the explanations.

I prove that the flat earth map is a north-polar azimuthal equidistant projection of the globe earth. This is why the southern continents such as Australia are so distorted, and why Antarctica is rendered as a white ring. The patent for the *Gleason's Map* tells you that it's a projection of the globe earth.

I address perspective, as this is a huge area of deception; because if the earth were flat, we would see things very differently. For instance, a common flat earth saying is that *'the horizon always rises to meet our eyes,'* but you can use the Theodolite app on your phone, to prove it wrong.

I give simple tips on how the sun and moon both prove that the earth is a globe. Once you understand the perspective deceptions that are given on flat-earther videos, you'll see that the sun and moon are faithful witnesses of a globe earth.

I disprove that the moon illuminates itself and explain why people believe that moonlight is colder. I provide simple things that you can do to prove it out for yourself; instead of trusting explanations on videos.

The book resource page is **FlatEarthDeception.com/resources**

Geocentricity Books

I've given basic overviews of the geocentric view, but these books provide much more information for you to study.

Geocentrism 101: An Introduction into the Science of Geocentric Cosmology by Robert A. Sungenis, PhD

Geocentrism 102: An Introduction into the History of the Church versus Galileo by Robert A. Sungenis, PhD

Galileo Was Wrong by Robert A. Sungenis, PhD

In Search of the Beginning – A Seeker's Journey to the Origin of the Universe, Life and Man by Dean Davis.

Geocentricity: Christianity in the Woodshed by Gerardus D. Bouw, Ph.D. The successor to *Geocentricity* and its predecessor, *With Every Wind of Doctrine*.

He Maketh His Sun to Rise: A Look at Biblical Geocentricity, by Dr. Thomas M. Strouse, Dean of Bible Baptist Theological Seminary

The Bible and Geocentricity, by James N. Hanson, Professor Emeritus of the Cleveland State University

Book References

The Firmament/Dome/Vaulted Dome

1 - Morris, Henry, Scientific Creationism, 1984, p. 211.
2 - http://blog.try-god.org/tag/al-ruccaba/

Geocentric Earth Findings

1 - I. Bernard Cohen, Birth of a New Physics, revised and updated, 1985, p. 78.
2 - Albert A. Michelson, "The Relative Motion of the Earth and the Luminiferous Ether," American Journal of Science, Vol. 22, August 1881, p. 125
3 - Arthur Eddington, The Nature of the Physical World, 1929, pp. 11
4 - The Theory of Relativity, 1958, p. 4
5 - Science in History: Volume 3, p. 744, from Jaffe, p.88
6 - Historian Lincoln Barnett, The Universe and Dr. Einstein, p. 44.
7 - Historian Lincoln Barnett, The Universe and Dr. Einstein, p. 73
8 - G.J. Whitrow, The Structure and Evolution of the Universe, 1949, p. 79
9 - Bernard Jaffe, Michelson and the Speed of Light, 1960, p. 76
10 - Modern Physics and Antiphysics, p. 54
11 - Physicist, Lawrence Krauss "The Energy of Empty Space That Isn't Zero".
12 - Y. P. Varshni, "The Red Shift Hypothesis for Quasars: Is the Earth the Center of the Universe?" Astrophysics and Space Science 43 (1): 3 (1976).
13 - Jonathan Katz, The Biggest Bangs, p. 111.
14 - The Evolution of Physics: From Early Concepts to Relativity and Quanta, Albert Einstein and Leopold Infeld, 1938, 1966, p. 212.
15 - James A. Coleman, Relativity for the Layman, p. 37
16 - George Ellis, Scientific American, "Thinking Globally, Acting Universally"
17 - Dean Davis, In Search of the Beginning
18 - New York Times, July 11, 1935. P. 23, c.8
19 - Stephen Hawking, The Grand Design, pages 41-42.

The Deception About Earth's Orientation

1 - General Montholon, Memorial of the Captivity of Napoleon, pp. 62, 174.
2 - Prefaces and prologues to famous books, Volume 39, p. 52
3 - Martin Luther, Luther's Works. Vol 54. Table Talk, (Fortress Press, 1967), 358–9.
4 - John Calvin: A Sixteenth-Century Portrait
5 - MacDonnell, Joseph. Companions of Jesuits: A Tradition of Collaboration. Fairfield, CT: Fairfield University Press, 1995.65.
6 - How the Catholic Church Built Western Civilization, Thomas Woods Jr. p. 111
7 – Reuters News Service, Lifestyle October 28, 2014

David Nikao Flat Earth Deception Website

FlatEarthDeception.com – This website gives logical explanations which you can use to prove out the shape of the earth.

FlatEarthDeception.com/resources is the book resource page.

FlatEarthDeception.com/feedback is the book feedback page.

David Nikao Prophecy Fulfillment Websites

70thWeekOfDaniel.com – This Bible study series explains the fulfillment of the 70 weeks of Daniel 9 prophecy, with the focus being on the 70th week, as it points to Messiah's first advent.

TheOlivetDiscourse.com – This Bible study series explains how Messiah's prophecies in His Olivet Discourse in Matthew 24, Mark 13 and Luke 21, are fulfilled.

RevelationTimelineDecoded.com - This Bible study series explains the fulfillment of the seals, trumpets, bowls, the little book, the two witnesses, the antichrist beast, the false prophet, and the harlot who is called *"Mystery, Babylon the Great."*

"He which testifieth these things saith, Surely I come quickly. Amen. Even so, come, Lord Jesus. The grace of our Lord Jesus Christ be with you all. Amen."
Revelation 22:20-21

Made in United States
Orlando, FL
11 October 2022